D1714924

Vacation Under the Sicilian Sun

by Remo Faieta, Ph.D.

DORRANCE
PUBLISHING CO
EST. 1920
PITTSBURGH, PENNSYLVANIA 15238

The contents of this work, including, but not limited to, the accuracy of events, people, and places depicted; opinions expressed; permission to use previously published materials included; and any advice given or actions advocated are solely the responsibility of the author, who assumes all liability for said work and indemnifies the publisher against any claims stemming from publication of the work.

Dorrance Publishing Co
585 Alpha Drive
Pittsburgh, PA 15238
Visit our website at *www.dorrancebookstore.com*

ISBN: 978-1-6470-2011-8
eISBN: 978-1-6470-2030-9

Contents

Preface

During a Christmas Holiday, while dining in an Italian restaurant. Paul: "Honey, where do you like to go for our next summer vacation?"

Angela: "Sweetheart, nowhere else but Sicily, and let me tell you why."

"I heard and read so much about Sicily that the desire of visiting it has been on my mind for a long time. I love to be on an island with a blue sea, radiant sun, clear sky, star-studded nights, mild weather, scenic panoramas, mountains, landscapes with fields of golden wheat, rows of vineyards, orchards of olive, orange and lemon trees. I dream of relaxing in pristine sandy beaches, walking in charming pebbly bays, hiking on mountain paths, sitting by the boardwalk of quaint seashore villages."

"Through my high school and college years, I was fascinated by the Greek and Roman history and culture. I love to see and touch historic sites with ancient temples, amphitheaters, monuments, and ruins. I am also fond of medieval and baroque history and architecture. I like to see castles, old churches, and palaces with rich mosaic art works, hilltop towns untouched by time, cobblestone streets. I want to meet local people, sit in rustic restaurants, and enjoy good food and wine. Visiting an active volcano is also in my list."

"Darling, Sicily has all of that. Moreover, don't forget that I have family roots in the Sunny Island. It has always been my dream to visit the little town where my grandparents came from. Let's make our next vacation a unique, relaxing, educational, and emotional experience.

"Yes, Honey! Let's begin planning our trip. Let's look for an escorted group tour, because with it we are safer, we can make new friends, have more fun, and most of all, we can have peace of mind."

Chapter 1

SICILY: A BEAUTIFUL ISLAND

An ancient legend says that when God created the world, He took a *gem* from his crown and dropped it in the Mediterranean Sea. That gem became a beautiful island, the island of Sicily (Sicilia). Ever since the gem has shined so brightly that whoever saw it loved it and wanted to own it.

Sicily is the largest, most fertile, and most populated island in the Mediterranean Sea. It is entirely wrapped in a crystal-clear blue sea, like a pretty blue ribbon. Size-wise it is comparable to the State of Massachusetts. It has a population of five million people. Because of its triangular shape, in the ancient times, it was called *Tinacria* (island with three corners). Today, the Sicilians call it *Sicilia Bedda* (Beautiful Sicily) and others refer to it as *L'Isola del Sole* (The Sunny Island), because it does not know a day without sun.

Nature has endowed Sicily with countless gifts: sunny days, mild climate, mountains, rolling hills, scenic landscapes, sandy beaches, large fields of wheat, endless rows of vineyards, groves of olives and fruit trees. With more than 2,000 hours of sunshine per year, the Sicilian sky has the European record of luminosity. With its spectacular trails of fire, lava, and snow, Mt. Etna gives the island a unique mark of beauty and prestige. Moreover, Sicilia Bedda has an abundance of magnificent historic sites and a large variety of culinary delights.

Dear Reader, I know you are eager to go through the next chapters of this book and discover the uniqueness of the Sunny Island, but, before you do that, let me tell you what that island looks like and who were the people who owned it. Let's briefly survey its coastline and hinterland and let's do it in mid-May, the best time to be in Sicily.

We explore the coastline by flying a small airplane. Let's go counterclockwise, flying from Palermo to Trapani, and from there, to Agrigento, Siracusa, Catania, Taormina, Messina, and Cefalu'. Ready? What do we see? The Palermo area is just unique, spectacular. On three sides we see mountains that surround a very large plain known as *La Conca d'Oro* (The Golden Shell), filled with orange trees. On the north side we see the blue Tyrrhenian Sea. The magic city of Palermo lies in that charming shell. We see also the pristine sandy beach of Mondello and a few fishing villages. What a view!

CARRETTO: symbol of Sicily

Continuing towards Trapani, we find a landscape with high craggy mountains and then we see vast fields of vineyards and olive groves that resemble a chess board. Enchanting little bays, small and relaxing sandy beaches, tiny pebbly coves, dramatic coastal rocks and picturesque villages with colorful fishing boats can be seen along the shoreline. The quaint city of Castellammare del Golfo, the medieval town of Erice, and the sandy beach of San Vito Lo Capo are just unforgettable.

We continue our flight along the southern coast which spans from Trapani to south of Syracuse. We see a long stretch of majestic coastline made of jagged highlands overlooking the turquoise sea, white sandy beaches and wind-dunes. Vast undulating hills covered with wheat, vineyards, olive, carob, and almond trees are seen everywhere. In this setting we must mention the Marsala area, famous for its sweet wines, Mazara del Vallo, known for its golden beach, and Agrigento, renowned for its ancient temples.

Flying over the Iblei Mountains of south-east Sicily we regret that there is no airport in this area. We would love to visit Ragusa and Modica with their mixture of splendid ancient dwellings and baroque churches and palaces. We would also like to walk on the hills covered with vast fields of vineyards, olive, almond, carob and orange trees. That entire area looks like a work of art.

When our small airplane reaches the Catania area we have a pleasant surprise: the entire region is dominated by the majestic Mt. Etna, relentlessly spitting fire and smoke and snowcapped most of the year. Then, looking down from our airplane, we see an immense plain completely covered with fields of orange and lemon trees. Finally, from Taormina to Messina, we find cliffs of black lava descending all the way to the Ionian Sea. We see also many picturesque fishing villages.

SICILIAN COAST

Flying along the northern Sicilian coastline, we encounter the city of Messina and its Strait with commercial and cruise ships. Then we continue westward and discover the Nebrodi and Madonie mountains on the left and the blue Tyrrhenian Sea on the right. The terrain there is characterized by a variety of landscapes comprising woody mountain peaks, gentle slopes, cliffs going straight to the sea, wide creeks and coves, pebbled beaches, small fields with orange and olive trees, vegetable gardens, cactuses, and palm trees. Numerous medieval towns and castles are seen on hilltops, while all construction along the coast is modern and has fashionable seaside resorts. It would be interesting to stop and visit the picturesque towns of Tindari, Patti, Gioiosa Marea, Brolo, Sant'Agata di Militello, and, most of all, Cefalu'.

After traveling along the entire Sicilian coastline, we can definitely say: *it is beautiful!* But Sicily is not made only of coastlines. The Sunny Island has also an extensive hinterland, which is no less beautiful and no less interesting. Let's explore that too and this time let's travel by car, driving through a country road that goes up from Termini Imerese to the province of Enna and Caltanisetta.

Proceeding from the blue coast to the hinterland, we are surprised to see how quickly the plain, dotted with vegetable and fruit groves, is replaced by steep hillsides, cliffs, canyons, and valleys. Then, as we climb higher, at every turn of the road, we encounter a succession of undulating hills covered with vast fields of wheat that shine like gold under the sun. Reaching the highest elevation, the panoramic view becomes wider and the eye wanders over immense plateaus with large meadows of hay, blood-red poppies, yellow mustard, and sunflowers. Down in the valleys we can see verdant pastures with cattle, horses and flocks of sheep grazing peacefully. A few small ponds dot the upper landscape. In the distance, jagged mountain peaks enhance the beauty of hinterland Sicily.

Most of those highlands are completely devoid of trees, except along the streams down in the valleys. Only a few solitary and old farm houses are seen in the countryside. People in the hinterland live in medieval towns perched atop rocky crags, clung on a bare hilltop or nestled in the hollow of a rocky hill. The panoramic view from those towns takes one's breath away: from there one can see other towns on distant hills and large fields covered with golden wheat. At times the villages and their castles are wrapped in a mist and seem to be floating over the clouds. It is just picturesque, impressive, spectacular!

Those medieval hillside towns are untouched by time and keep their traditions, folklore, and strong family ties. There, one feels in close contact with nature and finds the most authentic Sicilian life style. There, one can get in touch with the locals in a spontaneous way and enjoy their hospitality and good food. For that purpose one should visit any of these towns: Polizzi Generosa, Calascibetta, Caltabellotta, Gangi, Petralia, Prizzi, Caccamo, Butera, Castro-nuovo, Centuripe, Aidone, Barrafranca, Mussomeli, Agira, Pollina, Caltabel-lotta, etc. After this brief survey of the Sicilian coast and hinterland, we can certainly say that *Bella Sicilia has it all!*

CALASCIBETTA, A TYPICAL HINTERLAND TOWN

Because of its natural beauty and strategic location, the Sunny Island has known waves after waves of conquerors and has been ruled by every ethnic group living along the Mediterranean coast and beyond. Therefore, now let's find out who were those people. Since the Italian peninsula is only two miles away, one would think that Sicily has been *Italian* since the remote times. That is wrong! Sicily has been Italian only since the year 1860!

The origins of Bella Sicilia go back to prehistory. It is believed that its ear-liest inhabitants were the *Sicanians*, originating from Africa. They settled in the central part of Sicily. The *Elymians* came from the Middle East and occu-pied the western part. The *Sicels* inhabited the eastern part of the island and gave it the name of Sicily. We know very little about those people.

5

The *Phoenicians*, a great maritime people from today's Lebanon, came to Sicily around the year 1000 B.C. They founded the city of Panormus (Palermo). Attracted by their prosperity, the powerful *Greeks* came to the island around the year 800 B.C. and owned it for 600 years. They battled against the indigenous populations and imposed their own culture, language, religion, philosophy, laws, costumes, and arts. They founded numerous cities among which Messina, Siracusa, Gela, Selinunte and Imera. With the Greeks, Sicily knew a long period of development and prosperity. They built stupendous temples and monuments that even today surprise the visitors.

The Greeks' success caused concern for the beautiful, wealthy, civilized, and powerful city of *Carthage* on the northern coast of Africa. The Greeks and the Carthaginians fought fiercely for the possession of Sicily. Next, with the pretext of protecting the Greeks, the *Romans* seized, colonized, and controlled the Sunny Island for almost 1,000 years. They too imposed their language, built cities, and brought prosperity to the Island.

When the Roman Empire fell, the *Vandals and Goths*, barbarian tribes from north Europe, invaded and ruled Sicily for about 200 years. They were then driven out by the *Byzantines*, people from the east side of the Mediterranean Sea. These people owned Sicily for the next 300 years.

The Carthaginians, now known as *Arabs*, invaded Sicily again in 827 A.D. and possessed it for 200 years. They too brought prosperity by introducing agricultural innovations, promoting arts, science, and commerce. They constructed magnificent palaces and monuments. Palermo, seat of the Emirs, became such a splendid city that it rivaled in prestige with Bagdad, Cairo and Damascus. Although under the Arab domination Greek and Latin language were tolerated, Arabic became the official language in the island. Even today many Sicilians have a family name with the Arabic word *Allah* (God): Zappala', Badala', Fragala', Vadala', etc. Several Sicilian cities and towns still contain the Arabic word *Kalt*, which means *Fortress*: Caltanisetta, Caltabellotta, Caltagirone, Caltavuturo, etc.

In 1091 the Arabs were overthrown by the *Normans*, a people from northwest France; they owned Sicily for the next 200 years. Through marriage inheritance, later the island fell under the dominion of the *Swabians*, a Germanic tribe. They owned Sicily from 1194 to 1268. Both the Normans and Swabians brought additional prosperity to the island and built many castles, palaces, and churches that are still intact and astound us today. Next, it was *France's* turn to control Sicily, but they were quickly ousted by the *Spaniards* in 1282. Spain possessed Sicily until 1712, more than 400 years. Alas, because of their careless and despotic government, under the Spaniards that shining *Sicilian Gem* became completely tarnished!

From 1713 to 1735 Sicily became a possession of the House of Savoy, of the Austrians, and of the Bourbons of Naples. The Bourbons ruled it for more than 100 years. Finally, in 1860 the *King of Savoy* made of it a part of the newly formed Kingdom of Italy.

The Phoenicians, Carthaginians, Greeks, Romans, Barbarians, Byzantines, Arabs, Normans, Swabians, French, Spaniards, Savoy, Austrians, Bourbons, and finally the Italians: they all fought to own *Bella Sicilia*! Mamma Mia! Is there any wonder why? Well, the Swabian Emperor Frederick II tells us why: "I do not envy God's Paradise, because I am satisfied to live in Sicily!"

Because so many different ethnic people owned Sicily, the history of that island might sound like a fantasy tale, but it is not so! Each of those people left in the island something of themselves. They left indelible marks, as we can still see in the ruins, temples, ancient amphitheaters, theaters, architecture, cathedrals, churches, palaces, mosaics, arts, language, costumes, songs, poetry, folklore, tales, literature, proverbs, music, and food. All those marks accumulated one on top of the other, melted together, and gave life to a unique civilization, the Sicilian Civilization. Today, Sicily is a world by itself, a world with its own history, its own personality, and its own soul. Yes, the entire Sicilian Island can be considered as a marvelous museum. Touring it is like having its history unfolding at our feet. And that is what we are going to discover in this book.

FIGHTING FOR THE CONQUEST OF SICILY

7

Chapter 2

GOING ON VACATION TO SUNNY SICILY

Dear Reader, greetings to you! My name is Remo Faieta. I have been organizing and escorting *Group Tours* to Italy for the past many years. Most tours covered north and central Italy; others covered central and south Italy and that means the regions of Abruzzo, Campania, Puglia, Basilicata, Calabria, and Sicily. A few tours covered only Sicily. *In this book I describe a group tour that took place only in Sicily.* Please join my vacationers and find out what an *Escorted Tour to the Beautiful and Sunny Sicily* is all about. You will feel like if you actually were on tour with us. 1)

For the Sicily Tour described herein, I had a group of 27 enthusiast people; most of them from Ohio and Pennsylvania. Their average age was 50. They were not ordinary vacationers, but a group of lively people eager to discover the Sunny Island and have a good time. Some of them were more than enthusiast: they had family roots there. All of them had one thing in mind: to travel throughout Sicily, discover its natural beauty, visit its ancient sights, learn about its history and culture, eat good food, drink fine wine, dance, and have fun every day. Nobody was on a diet, for sure!

---

1) It is important to understand here that this book is not a *Guide Book*. People in an escorted tour don't need a guide book, because they have their own *Live Guide!* The purpose of this book is to give the Reader a good overview of what an escorted group tour to Sicily is all about and the fun associated with it.

Yes, those people were truly *on vacation* and let me tell you what that means. The term "vacation" comes from the Latin verb "vacare", which means "to vacate, to make empty". Therefore, to be on vacation and to enjoy it one has to "vacate, make empty" his/her mind of all daily concerns at home. Then, one has to fill that empty mind with *new and pleasurable things.* People going on a vacation are called "vacationers". Oh, for sure, Sicily has plenty of new and pleasurable things to offer, as we are going to see in this book!

After months of preparation, in early May 2016, we were off on our adventure. We all met at the Airport of Newark, N.J. When I arrived there, I went straight to Gate D17 and I found a large number of travelers waiting to go to Rome, Italy. Among them, which ones belonged to my group? I had met only a few of them. Since in my instructions I had informed them to look for a man with a *red cap* holding a *red carnation* atop an antenna, when I raised that sign, several smiling people got up and greeted me, "Hello! You must be Remo. Glad to meet you." Rose, a pretty single woman, approached me and said, "You have beautiful twinkling blue eyes and a big smile. Are you really from Italy?" I kindly responded, "Grazie, Rose." At the same time I looked around and thought, "I hope no one heard her!" Time passed quickly as I answered questions. At 5:45, our airplane took off for Rome, Italy.

The overnight flight was pleasant. We had dinner, watched movies, and dozed now and then. At 8:00 a.m., we landed in Rome. Although we were all weary, an air of happiness could be read on everybody's face. We picked up our baggage and went through the customs. The officers stamped our passports and smiled.

"Oh, look at those young policemen; aren't they cute?" said a couple of my excited young ladies. Laura remarked, "We are no longer in America. Everybody here speaks Italian!" "Wow, can you smell the aroma of the espresso coffee?" said Luisa.

We waited about two hours at Fiumicino Airport and then boarded the Ryanair for Palermo. We flew for one hour over the blue Tyrrhenian Sea. As the plane approached Sicily, people began to feel like they were landing into a magic land of legends.

After picking up our baggage, I called the roll and said, "Ok. Everyone is here. Now follow me to the bus!" Everybody grabbed their luggage and followed me with firm steps, like soldiers on a military parade. The walk to the bus parking lot was short. I instructed everyone to leave all baggage on both sides of the bus, to take a seat inside and relax. Our bus had 55 blue and plush seats, large windows, overhead temperature and sound controls, a bathroom, coffee maker, and a microphone. For the next several days, that bus became our home away from home.

With the exception of a few couples, my "Good Sheep", as I used to call my vacationers, they did not know each other. They sat on the bus silently and smiling. Then, I entered the bus, picked up the microphone, faced them and said, "Buon Giorno a voi tutti (Good morning everybody) and welcome to Bella Sicilia! How nice to see these smiling faces! I am *Remo*, your tour director. I will be with you for the rest of the tour. And this young man is *Corporal Giuseppe*, our bus driver." I liked to tease Giuseppe by calling him *Corporal*, but after a few days people promoted him to *Captain Giuseppe*. There was an immediate response from the group. "Hello, Remo! Buon Giorno, Corporal Giuseppe!" Although most people had never met the others in the group, immediately they became buddies or *cumpari*, as they say in Sicily. The bus started rolling and our fabulous Sicilian adventure began.

We took the freeway running on a narrow stretch of land between the sea on the left and Mount Cuccio on the right. We drove by the town of Carini and Capaci. We passed through the outskirts of Palermo, Bagheria, and Termini Imerese. I gave some information about those cities. Finally, we arrived at our deluxe *Fiesta Hotel*, right by the beach. There were three other tour buses, one from Lecce (south-east Italy) and two from Germany. The hotel had a large tropical garden and two large outdoor swimming pools. Right after checking-in, my youngest people went to explore the garden, while the others sat at the bar or took a nap in their room.

At 7:30 p.m., everybody came to the dining room, where many other guests were already eating. A few of my ladies and gentlemen were dressed like kings and queens; they smiled to everybody. When we saw people coming back to their table holding dishes loaded with delicious food, we understood it was a self-service.

The restaurant was large and impressive. On the right side of the food area, we found the hot food section with three kinds of pasta, three kinds of meat, two kinds of chicken, and two kinds of fish. In the middle of the room, there was a huge display of antipasto, salads, diet and gluten-free food. On the left side we found at least ten different kinds of mouthwatering desserts, among which the Sicilian *cannoli* were the most popular. A glass wall separated the front of the kitchen from the food area. We could see the cooks very busy preparing the smoking and delicious food right in front of us. They wore white uniforms and tall, white hats.

We were allowed to eat anything and as much as we wanted. Wine was not included with the cost of dinner, but that did not deter anyone from enjoying it, since most tables had bottles of wine. Now and then a loud *Salute!* (Cheers) resounded in the dining room. Mamma Mia, it was a real fiesta of food, a very pleasant first-hand touch with the Sicilian life!

During dinner two men and a woman, dressed in Sicilian folkloric clothes, came to the dining room and entertained us with music and songs. A few people got up and danced *Tarantella*. The musicians invited us to stop at the hotel's open terrace and dance under the moonlight. Grazie (Thank You), but we were too tired that first night; most of us went to sleep. Buona Notte! (Good Night).

OUR LIVELY GROUP

Chapter 3

PALERMO, A CITY WITH ARTISTIC WONDERS

PALERMO

In the morning of day three of our tour, at 6:30 a.m. everybody's phone chimed: ring, ring, ring. I rolled out of bed, opened the window, looked outside and enjoyed a spectacular view. The sun was rising in the horizon, right above the Tyrrhenian Sea and its golden rays, reflecting on the glittering water, made it look like if the water was on fire. Next to my room I heard Tony sing, "*O Sole Mio....*"

Waiting for the restaurant to open, a few "early birds" were slowly walking in the tropical garden; they touched the beautiful pink rhododendron in full blossom. At about 8:00 a.m., most of my "Good Sheep" were in the restaurant; many were eating at tables set outside under palm trees. We had a fabulous buffet-breakfast.

Kelly came in singing, "It's such a pretty day today. Look at the sunshine!" The temperature was in the high 70s and the sky striking blue. Everybody was in a festive mood and eager to begin the Sicilian adventure. Although good food and fun were important ingredients to enliven our adventure, discovering the island's artistic and historic riches was on everybody's mind. They made me think of the high-spirited horses ready to start their race in the ancient Roman stadiums!

At 9:00 a.m., our bus began to roll. *Evelyn* volunteered to say a short prayer every morning. Later, we called her, "Sister Evelyn". Before getting onto the freeway, we had to pass under a low bridge. I said jokingly, "Duck in, so the bus can make it!" Surprisingly, many did duck in; they liked to humor me. We were headed for Palermo, the capital of the Sunny Island that encloses all the magic of Sicily. Its long history is still engraved in its monuments, cobblestone streets, aromas, and flavors of the cuisine.

Palermo, a bustling city of about one million people, is picturesquely located in a plain between mountains and sea. That entire area was once called the *Golden Shell*, a beautiful and fertile plain with fields of orange and lemon trees. Recently most of that Shell has been transformed into modern urban developments. Tourists have no interest whatsoever in modern Palermo. They want to see the city's historic center, which has maintained the original medieval uniqueness with an intricate maze of closed alleys, narrow streets, fountains, and small squares. It is in that area that one can find palaces, monuments, and baroque churches dating back to the time of the Arab, Norman, and Spanish domination. Walking downtown Palermo today, one can relive its history and learn about the many different people that dominated the city and the entire island.

At 9:30 a.m., our *Corporal Giuseppe* dropped us off in front of an old, reddish palace with an unusual architecture. There we found many tourists standing in line to go inside. My good friend *Larry (Lorenzo) Lo Iacono*, an Italian-American from Findlay, Ohio, was waiting for us. He moved to Palermo in 2008 as an English teacher. Any time I take a group of Americans to Palermo, he is overjoyed to be our guide. He is very knowledgeable of the city and the island.

Lorenzo greeted us and explained, "This massive building is the *Norman Palace* founded by King Roger II. It was built on the ruins of an Arab castle. Look at this inscription on the wall; it is written in Latin, Greek, and Arabic and it states that the palace was built in 1145 A.D. It was used as kings' residence for many centuries. Today, it is a museum."

Then, Lorenzo took us inside the superb courtyard with three rows of superimposed arches. On the ground floor, by a large staircase, we admired an old horse-drawn carriage used by the kings. It looks just like the coaches we see in fantasy movies. Our guide walked us to the second floor and showed the Royal Apartments, the Audience Hall, and the Red Hall, all sumptuously decorated with vivid mosaics depicting hunting scenes.

Next, Lorenzo took us into the main attraction of the Palace: the Kings' private chapel, called *Palatine Chapel*, a true architectural jewel. It is decorated with Byzantine, Arabic, and Norman glittering mosaics from the 11th century. Those mosaics are considered to be among the most beautiful in the world.

When we entered the chapel, we felt like entering the kingdom of fairytales. At first we stood there astounded, with lumps in our throat to see the sheer power and beauty of the place. Then we looked all around with amazement: every single inch in the walls, ceiling, and dome is covered with the most stunning, glittering, and splendid mosaics, all set on a blazing gold background. Even the floor is made of mosaics with marble inlays. The French writer Guy de Maupassant defined it as "The most beautiful jewel ever dreamed by men".

The bright mosaics depict historic events and biblical scenes, starting with the Genesis, the story of Noah and the Ark, the story of Jacob with angels running up and down the ladder, and so on. The New Testament mosaic scenes include the apostles, saints, and angels. There is an amazing depiction of the baptism of Christ with the water swirling around his body in wavy of gold leaves. Of particular beauty are the spectacular mosaics portraying the Blessing Savior above the main Altar. Lorenzo gave us a thorough explanation of everything we saw.

Some of us sat alone in the chapel in contemplation of the wonder of it all. We could almost hear the steps of King Roger slowly walking to his throne at the end of the chapel. We imagined seeing also the king's entourage dressed in fashionable clothes, the religious procession, the grey-haired priests bowing and genuflecting at the altar, the organ playing, and the people chanting.

Although the mosaic scenes were made 900 years ago, they look as if they were done recently. They still evoke the grandeur that Palermo enjoyed under the Norman domination. Art lovers and daydreamers yearn to see the Palatine Chapel. For us, seeing it was a real walk through the Bible. It was both an educational and emotional experience. One does not have to be religious to be moved by those images and by the spirituality they express.

PALATINE CHAPEL

We left the Norman Palace and walked by a group of elderly men playing cards under a huge palm tree. They did not look at us; they were used to see crowds of tourists. When we came in front of a massive city gate, called *Porta Nuova* (New Gate), Bruno shouted, "Holly Molly, what happened to those men?" Lorenzo explained, "This is the main entrance gate to the historic center of Palermo. It was built in 1535 to celebrate the conquest of Tunis, in Africa, by Charles V, King of Spain and Sicily. The four gigantic statues you see in the front of the gate represent the captured Moor soldiers. Look, two of them are chained up and the other two have both hands cut off. Poor men!"

We walked under Porta Nuova and entered *Corso Vittorio Emanuele*, which is Palermo's main street. It was busy with locals, University students, and tourists. That street has many stores selling all kinds of souvenirs, especially copies

15

of the colorful *Pupi* (puppets) and the traditional *Carretto Siciliano* (Sicilian cart). The Pupi are hand-made marionettes used in small theaters and represent chivalrous medieval events, classical myths, biblical stories, and heroic deeds of Charlemagne's paladins. The Carretto, drawn by a well adorned donkey, is made of fine wood and is brightly painted with images depicting scenes of Sicilian history, medieval heroic actions, and folkloric scenes. In the olden times, the Pupi and the Carretto served the purpose of conveying historic information to the illiterate people.

Suddenly, we came face to face with a grandiose, elegant, and brownish building with various architectural styles; it looked like a fortress. Lorenzo told us that we were actually in front of the famous *Cathedral of Palermo*, built in 1185.

"Imagine", he said, "originally this enormous building was a pagan temple, then, it became a Christian Basilica. When the Arabs took Palermo, they changed it into a splendid mosque. With the advent of the Normans, the mosque was modified to the present form and consecrated as Christian church again. That is why the outside has an unusual appearance with a mixture of Roman, Arab, Norman, and medieval architecture. Look here, a passage of the Koran is still engraved in the column by the left entrance door. This Cathedral served also as coronation site of many kings: Norman, Catalan, Swabian, Spanish, and Savoy kings. Yes, Palermo speaks of its history through this monumental Cathedral."

"Mary, do you believe that many different ethnic kings ruled in Sicily?" asked Lorenzo.

"I really don't know; it seems like a fairy-tale", she replied.

"Well, look to your left. There you see the porphyry tombs of the Norman Kings and queens who ruled Sicily: *Roger II* (died in 1154), *Frederic II* of Hohenstaufen (died in 1250), *Henry VI* (Emperor of Germany and son of Frederick Barbarossa, died in 1197), and *Queen Constance* (died in 1222). The remains of *Saint Rosalia*, patron of Palermo, are contained in a silver urn in the chapel at the end of the right nave. If you go to the crypt of this church, you can see many other tombs of royalties and Sicilian nobility. You can also see the priceless crown of Queen Constance decorated with the most precious gems, pearls, sapphires, and golden embroidery." What a history lesson!

PALERMO: CATHEDRAL

From the Cathedral, we strolled on Main Street, passed by many splendid palaces and churches dating back to the Spanish domination. At Piazza Bologna, we saw the statue of King Charles V of Spain. Then, we turned right and walked in a maze of old, narrow, and winding streets that were once the center of an old Arab quarter.

Soon we found ourselves walking right into a vast and colorful outdoor market where locals go for their daily shopping. The market is called *Ballaro'*. It has been in existence in that same place since the time of the Arab domination, more than 1,000 years ago. The market snakes through a few city blocks and is characterized by a splendid display of fruit, vegetables, bread, meat, fish, swordfish, giant octopus, clothes, leather goods, house wares, etc. Reluctantly, we passed by cut-off heads of cows, horses, and goats. Plucked chickens and skinned rabbits were also on display. The place resounded with thunderous voices of vendors hollering, shouting, selling, laughing, and eating. Betty, too busy licking a *gelato* (ice cream), came a few inches from bumping her head against the cut-off head of a goat hanging from a rusty hook. "Oh, my God!" she screamed and jumped back.

At the end of the market we found a few blacksmith and carpenter workshops. We could hear a blacksmith striking his anvil. A bicycle repairman was using a table and a chair as office on the street. Another man, sitting by a table, was selling wine by the glass. An elderly man sitting on a knife-grinder was chanting an old song, while sharpening knives and scissors. He gladly posed for a picture with Nancy, but then with a dusty finger, he pointed to his cheek for a kiss. Immediately Nancy rewarded him, but then she wiped her lips. Mario got our attention when he shouted, "Holy smoke, look up there!" He had just spotted a beautiful brunette on the second floor. She was hanging laundry on a clothes line stretched across her balcony. Mario waved at her and she blew a kiss to him. For a moment, he seemed transported in the realm of dreams! An elderly carpenter, wearing a dirty whitish apron, was in front of a shop making a table. Upon seeing us, he laid down his tools and kept on staring at our ladies. Luisa looked at him and shouted, "Hey, hey, Cumpare!" Yes, Ballaro' Market is an interesting open-air theater where one can experience the city's lively soul. We loved it!

BALLARO' MARKET

After we left Ballaro' Market, we passed by an old street sign written in Arabic, Hebrew, and Italian, evidence of Sicily's diverse past. Then, as we walked by a church, Paul said, "I have seen this church somewhere. Yes, I remember, it was featured in the movie *Godfather*". Lorenzo confirmed that and explained, "This is the Jesuit *Chiesa del Gesu'* (Church of Jesus) built in 1636. It is a masterpiece of the Baroque style. By *Baroque*, we mean an artistic technique that developed from the late 16th to the early 18th centuries. It was characterized by elaborate and flamboyant decorations, curves, and symmetrical designs, all intended to produce a feeling of drama and grandeur. *Extravagance* is the word that best describes the baroque style. It was applied in sculpture, painting, architecture, literature, dance, theater, and music."

"Understand that, although Sicily suffered a long period of economic deca-dence under the Spanish domination, everything pertaining to religion actually prospered. Palermo became adorned with numerous magnificent baroque churches and palaces. This Chiesa del Gesu' is one of them. From the outside, it does not look like anything special, but you know the saying, 'Don't judge a book by its cover'. Ok, now let's go inside and let's find out what baroque style really means."

When we opened the door and went inside, all we could say was "Wow!" We became astounded and speechless: the decor of that place was absolutely over-whelming, breathtaking. Once again, we felt we had entered a world of unleashed fantasy, a world of dreams. We were almost compelled to kneel in wonder. Our mind was blown away by the thousands of ornate marble carvings, lovely fres-coes, stucco works, paintings, mosaics, inlays, stained-glass windows, statues rep-resenting angels and saints, extravagant religious scenes, and more.

In addition to the usual religious designs, there were stucco and marble decorations, bas-reliefs, and sculptures of centaurs, unicorns, cherubs, dogs, horses, flowers, birds, animals, stained glasses, musical instruments, angels, sculptures, reliefs, thousands of baroque pieces, etc. Even the floor was made of colorful and shining marble with vivid inlays. Absolutely true, every single inch in that church was decorated with some form of elaborate ornamental art. What mostly impressed us was the opulence of artistic work in the ceiling: it had brilliant paintings that looked like a celestial glory. Certainly it could compete with the Sistine Chapel in Rome.

The overall impression of the baroque art inside the Chiesa del Gesu' was much to believe; it was a feast for the eyes that lifted our spirit. Words cannot describe it; one has to just go inside and see what baroque extravagance means. Moreover, it is amazing that, after more than 400 years, everything in that church is still untarnished!

While visiting the Chiesa del Gesu', some of my people, captivated by the beauty of that visual delight, sat on a bench and felt like crying. On the way out, Mike remarked, "I am not much of a religious person, but the view of this place has overwhelmed me. Yes, in a few minutes I have learned what baroque style is all about."

CHIESA DEL GESU': THE WALLS

Next, Lorenzo took us inside the church of *San Giuseppe dei Teatini* (St. Joseph of Teatini), built in 1612. "What can I say?" he commented. "It is another outstanding example of the Sicilian baroque, a true triumph of inlay marble art work. Know that in Palermo, we have many more artistic marvels. For example, if you could see the interior of Santa Caterina Church, once again you would be astounded before its mesmerizing baroque beauty. Well, we cannot see all of the churches today. I hope some time you can do that on your own. Now just take a few minutes to admire this marvel."

Yes, we found San Giuseppe dei Teatini astounding and mesmerizing! It was more than a *church*; it was a magnificent museum and it was 500-years-old! As we entered it, my enthusiast 27 *Art Lovers* ran to every corner and took many pictures. What impressed us most was the opulence of the work in the ceiling: that too can compete with the Sistine Chapel in Rome!

Although the Spanish rulers were not concerned about the well-being of the Sicilians, they certainly did care to immortalize their own name. In the very busy and fashionable heart of Palermo, the Vittorio Emanuele Street intersects with Maqueda Street and forms a beautiful square called *Quattro Canti* (four corners). The Square has four elegant palaces, all of the same architectural baroque style. The façade of each palace has three levels. All first levels are decorated with a fountain, the second levels have statues of Spanish kings (Charles V, Philip II, Philip III and Philip IV), and the third levels contain the statue of saints. Those statues have been watching the locals for the past 400 years. Standing in that square one feels like being downtown Madrid!

Right behind one of those palaces stands the remarkable *Piazza Pretoria* built in 1581. The Square is adorned with a large fountain decorated with numerous nude statues of humans, mermaids, satyrs, tritons, sirens, pagan gods and goddesses, nymphs, and mythical creatures. The flagrant nudity of the statues representing men was too much for the local churchgoers who found them shocking, outrageous, and disgraceful. They renamed that entire square *Piazza della Vergogna* (Square of Shame). Furthermore, all male private parts were mysteriously chopped off. They say that one night the local nuns managed to do that job! Imagine: said Square lies right in front of the nuns' Convent of St. Catherine! Today, tourists stop by that fountain and have fun taking pictures of the mutilated statues. Nancy posed while pretending to chop off the missing *thing* of a statue representing a naked man!

SQUARE OF SHAME

Within two minute walk from the Square of Shame, Lorenzo took us to another gem of Palermo's past glory: the celebrated *Martorana Church*. We had just held our breath in the magnificent Palatine Chapel and in the Baroque

21

Chiesa del Gesu' and now we were astonished again in admiration as we saw the 900-year-old Martorana Chapel. Mamma Mia, what a thrilling day!

Upon entering La Martorana, we became enraptured by the richness of its spectacular interior covered with frescoes, mosaics, and decorations executed by Byzantine craftsmen with an Arabic flavor. The impact upon our eyes and mind was such that we did not know where to look first. We were in Paradise again! It was all about art, history, and faith. There wasn't an inch of the walls left without magnificent ornamentations, paintings, and frescoes with vivid colors. There were wonderful mosaics on golden backgrounds depicting numerous biblical images, prophets, saints, angels, and other historic scenes. Even the pavement was made of polychrome inlaid marble tiles and mosaics. Of particular interest was the mosaic depicting Roger II being crowned by Christ. Equally stunning was the image of Christ Pantocrator surrounded by archangels, apostles, saints, and prophets.

The visit to the Martorana Chapel was another touching lesson of history and art unfolding before our eyes: it was just beautiful, inspiring. Our mind could barely take it all in, especially when we think that, after 900 years, those mosaics are still bright. The Palatine Chapel, the Cathedral, the Chiesa del Gesu', and La Matorana are the highlights of Palermo's artistic genius. For us it was a walk into the medieval time.

MARTORANA

After La Martorana we came back to today's real life. We walked along the wide Via Maqueda lined with numerous shops and elegant palaces of the vanished nobility. On the way, Evelyn asked our guide, "Lorenzo, the artists that made those wonderful works of art must have been real geniuses. Why did they display their talents only in churches and not in museums?"

"Dear Lady", explained Lorenzo, "it is because at that time there were no museums. Those are a rather of recent creation. In fact the oldest museums came to life only about 300 years ago. Before that, all artists worked in churches. That is why today many old churches are considered veritable museums. Even people indifferent to religion find them fascinating and educational."

After 20 minutes of slow ambling, we were in front of a majestic new building, called *Teatro Massimo* (Theater Massimo). It is the biggest opera house in Italy and the third in Europe. The Teatro hosts mostly classical music, operas, and ballets. Its façade resembles a classic temple and its large flight of steps is the favorite meeting place for locals and tourists. The fans of the movie *Godfather III* love to sit on the steps, because that is where an assassin, trying to kill Michael Corleone, fatally hit his daughter instead.

Since our feet were tired, our Corporal Giuseppe picked us up by Teatro Massimo, drove by the Port, and then through the Favorita Park, a hunting ground for the past Bourbon kings. At the end of that wooded road, we found many luxury villas of the "belle époque" and gardens with tropical flowers. We were in Mondello, the summer residences of Palermo nobility during the 19th century. Mondello is also a popular seaside holiday resort with turquoise water, white sand beach, classy shops, and good restaurants.

It was lunch time, thus we stopped at the popular *Da Calogero* restaurant, right by the blue sea. They serve sea food, especially swordfish, spaghetti with shrimp, clams, mussels, and boiled octopus seasoned with lemon drops and olive oil. Oh, yes, at Da Calogero we had a festival of food complemented with delicious local wine!

AT CALOGERO

At the end of our lunch, Paul told us, "I belong to the 21st century gener-ation, but, besides the good octopus lunch I just had, nothing of the modern time interests me. Yet, today I loved walking downtown medieval Palermo and admiring its most precious works of art created hundreds of years ago. Those wonders spoke to my heart and to my mind. I feel I belong to the generation of those great artists."

After all that eating, we walked to a nearby square. There was a large and fanciful Merry-Go-Round. We went on a ride and had fun. Some people looked at us in a strange way. Well, who said that a Merry-Go-Round is only for kids? Next, walking on the sandy beach, we were tempted to jump in the water and have fun, but none of us had a swimming suit. We were content to just wet our feet in the warm water.

At Hotel Fiesta, when I went to the dining room and saw my people eating a large amount of food, I said, "Mamma Mia, are you eating again?"

"Didn't you tell us that we are on a *pleasurable vacation?* We eat now and diet when we go home", they laughed.

By the end of that day, my enthusiastic 27 vacationers learned about Palermo's history, admired mosaic and baroque works of art, ate delicious food, drank fine wine, walked on the beach, and enjoyed an evening of music and dancing. Not bad for the first day of our Sicilian holiday!

Chapter 4

PICTURESQUE CEFALU',
MAGNIFICENT MONREALE, EERIE CATACOMBS

On day four of our tour we slept a little longer and had a late breakfast. It was another bright and clear day. At 10:30 a.m., we drove for about 20 minutes on a country road along the Tyrrhenian coast framed by green hills with age-old trees and orange groves. We arrived to *Cefalu'*, a picturesque medieval seaside town filled with historic buildings. The city was founded by the Greeks about 2,500 years ago on a picturesque rocky headland projecting into the sea. Right on top of it overhangs a huge, rocky, and precipitous cliff. Because of its mild weather, neat sandy beach, narrow and cobbled medieval streets, cozy shops, and good restaurants, today Cefalu' has become a major Sicilian tourist destination. The town has about 25,000 inhabitants.

We entered Cefalu' on *Corso Ruggero* and walked slowly among buildings and palaces of the Renaissance period. At the end of the street we found the beautiful *Piazza del Duomo*, which is the social and religious center of the city. The Piazza has restaurants with inside and outside tables. There, I called everybody's attention, "Come closer." Betty put her hand on my shoulder and said, "Closer than this?"

Then I said, "We are in the heart of Cefalu'. Look up there, that old and magnificent church is the *Duomo*, masterpiece of the Norman architecture and symbol and glory of this town. It was built in 1131 by the enlightened Norman

King Roger II to fulfill a vow to God after his fleet was saved during a violent storm. Go inside; you will love it. It is now 11:30; you have one hour of free time." A few of my enthusiast vacationers went to see the Duomo, others browsed in shops, sat on a bench under palm trees and enjoyed a *gelato* (ice cream) and *cannoli*.

When we regrouped, we walked on *Via Carlo Ortolano*, lined with quaint shops. At the end of the street we turned left and stopped by a large café with outside tables, right in front of the beach. There were many tourists relaxing and watching the world go by.

Next, we strolled along the narrow *Via Vittorio Emanuele*, the main tourist street. There we found lovely boutiques selling souvenirs, ceramics, gold, jewels, and souvenirs. A funny thing happened on that street: while Anna was admiring a piece of ceramic, she suddenly grabbed her butt, bounced forward, and screamed, "Ouch!" Someone had just pinched her! Who did it? It could not be the elder German couple next to her. We suspected the chubby mailman, who had just come out of the shop with a sneer and disappeared in the crowd.

A popular tourist curiosity on Via Vittorio Emanuele is the *Lavatoio*, a medieval stone laundry-mat located several steps below the street level. The water, quite cold, comes from the mountains, runs under the town, gushes out of the foundation of an old building, and runs through several stone basins. Here, the women washed their clothes from medieval times until recently. Imagine dozens of women coming down with baskets of dirty clothes, kneeling in front of the stone basins, their hands in the cold water, soaping and scrubbing pants, dresses, socks, sheets, rubbing and wringing them, even in winter. It must have been a hard work. It must have been also a pleasant time for the women to share the daily news and gossip.

CEFALU'

27

As we hit the road again, Mary said, "Yesterday in Palermo, we discovered many wonderful places, but we did not see the jewel of all jewels, the famous *Duomo* (cathedral) *of Monreale*. I read somewhere that if a visitor goes to Palermo and does not see that Duomo, he goes as a man and returns as a donkey. I don't want to return as a donkey." Many others shouted, "Yeah. We don't want that either!" "Signore e Signori (Ladies and Gentlemen)", I said, "relax; that is exactly where we are going now!"

Monreale is a picturesque hill town overlooking the Golden Shell and the city of Palermo. The name is a contraction of "Monte-Reale" (Royal-Mountain). The town has a population of about 35,000 inhabitants. It is renowned for its Norman Duomo completely covered with the most fabulous mosaics. It was built in 1189, and ever since it has been considered as the most important artistic monument of Sicily.

The legend has it that one day, while resting under a carob tree, the Norman King William II had a vision: the Virgin Mary told him that there was a great amount of gold buried under that tree; he should take it to build a church in that same spot. The King did as told.

To build the church the King hired the best artists of his kingdom and many more from the Byzantine and the Arab world. What those artists accomplished is more a divine than a human work of art. True, the Palatine and Martorana Chapels we have already admired are spectacular, but the Duomo of Monreale is "the most beautiful church in the world", as many scholars called it. It is also known as "The Golden Temple", because it is almost completely covered with golden mosaics. We can also define it as the most beautiful "museum" in the world.

From the parking lot in Monreale, we climbed a few flights of steps and arrived to the top of the hill where we walked on a cobble-stoned street with many souvenir shops. Finally, we came face to face with the famous 800-year-old Duomo. From the outside it does not mean too much, but upon entering it, we were confronted with an awe-inspiring beauty. It was a feast for our eyes and mind. We became speechless, dazzled by the splendor of it all. We felt like we were entering heaven again. There are no appropriate words to describe that Duomo; let's call it "The Crown Jewel of Sicily, a Work of Divine Glory, a Labor of Divine Love, a Spectacular Wonder of the Norman Architecture" or simply let us call it "breathtaking!"

My people preferred to be on their own to discover and enjoy in silence the extraordinary splendor of that artistic miracle. No surprise that we could not find Evelyn: She was sitting on a back pew in deep contemplation, almost in ecstasy.

Why is the Duomo of Monreale so special? Because its walls and ceiling are completely covered with the most shimmering mosaic art works depicting a very large number of scenes of the Old and New Testaments. The entire Bible has been placed in there to convey a sense of learning of the biblical episodes and events. Nine hundred years ago, people were illiterate, but, walking along the length of that church and looking at those mosaic pictures, they could *read* the scriptures straight off the walls and learn about the Bible. In fact, that Duomo has been called also "The Bible of the Poor" and an "Open Bible".

All biblical mosaic pictures are placed upon a background of gold tiles. Imagine, they used 4,500 pounds of pure gold to narrate the history of Christianity! From the upper portion of the walls to the ceiling, every inch is covered with that precious metal and shimmering mosaics! Everything that shines in there is gold!

Thousands of square meters are covered with biblical scenes starting from the creation of the universe to the resurrection of Christ. Among the numerous mosaic scenes depicting the Old Testament, let's mention a few: God creating Earth, Adam and Eve, Cain killing his brother Abel, the Flood, Noah, Moses, the Tower of Babylon, Sodom and Gomorrah, the fight of Jacob with the Angel, the Sacrifice of Isaac, Prophets, and Patriarchs. The mosaics of the New Testament show scenes representing the Annunciation, the Birth of the Savior, his Childhood, Miracles, Death and Resurrection, the Virgin Mary, St. Peter, St. Paul, and other apostles. There is also a myriad of other figures representing Archangels, Cherubs, Seraphs, saints, virgins, kings, illustrious churchmen, historic events, animals, plants, decorations, artistic traditions, and religious symbolism. Many mosaics are accompanied by inscriptions in Latin and Greek. Our neck became sore as we gazed up at those scenes!

Dominating everything in the Duomo, above the main altar, is the huge and majestic mosaic figure of "Christ Pantocrator" (Christ the Almighty) on gold background with inscription in Greek and Latin. The size of the image is impressive: the entire figure measures 52-feet across and 28 high. The head alone measures 15-feet and the right hand 7-feet. The Lord's majestic and wide-open eyes follow the visitor everywhere in the church and seem to read deep into his soul.

A side chapel at the end of the right aisle contains a few royal tombs: William I rests in a deep-red porphyry tomb; William II, the founder of that fabulous Duomo, is in a white marble tomb; the heart of King Louis IX of France is kept there too; he died in Monreale in 1270 returning from a crusade. Along the wall we saw the tombs of Queen Margaret, mother of William II, and the tomb of his two brothers, Roger and Henry.

What a first-hand history and art lesson we learned in Monreale! It was better than learning it in any text book. We could have spent days discovering and admiring the many precious works of art in that Duomo.

MONREALE: DUOMO

It was getting late, but since most of my enthusiast "Art Lovers" wished to see the eerie *Capuchin Catacombs*, I felt a visit there was also part of their cultural experience in Palermo.

When I asked if anyone knew what the Catacombs are, Mario quickly responded, "Yes, I know. That is where the dead people live!" Well, not quite so, Mario! The Catacombs are underground rooms where the first Christians buried their dead people during the Roman persecutions. Obviously, once buried, we don't see the corpses in their current appearance. However, that is not the case in the Capuchin Catacombs and let me tell you why.

On Pindemonte Street, there is a public cemetery and next to it stands an old Franciscan Monastery with Catacombs where one can actually see thousands of dead people. There was no need for the Capuchin Friars to dig underground burial sites for fear of persecution, but, instead of burying their dead companions in the public cemetery, they preferred to keep them in an underground room (catacomb) where they could see them and meditate on mortality. In order to be preserved and displayed, the corpses were first placed in a dehydration cell for eight months, then they were washed with vinegar, and finally dressed up and placed in wooden coffins, in glass coffins, or in niches.

As the number of dead friars increased, the Catacombs had to be expanded, and for that they needed financial help. Many local wealthy people made donations. In return they requested to be buried in that same Catacomb, so their relatives could visit them, maintain the corpses, hold their hands, and join them in prayer. Soon it became a status symbol for the local nobles to be entombed in the Capuchin Catacombs. That practice continued for about 400 years, from 1533 to 1920. Over the centuries, the Catacombs were expanded even more. They were divided into sections for men, women, virgins, children, priests, monks, and professionals. Today, there are about 8,000 corpses in those Catacombs. Several plaques remind the visitor to meditate on mortality. The most striking plaque is the one warning, "We were as you are; you will be as we are".

We paid a small entrance fee, descended a few steps, and came face to face with that macabre spectacle. Two minutes later, Mary ran out whining, "Oh, my God! I cannot take it!" The rest of us walked among the dead. What did we see? We saw rows and rows of skeletons. They were seated, standing, in closed glass coffins, in open coffins, in shelves, hanging from the ceiling, or simply nailed on the walls. Many skulls atop stuffed skeletons seemed to look at us with grinning eyes, admonishing that whoever we think we are, we all end up the same when we die.

The corpses nailed on the walls look very spooky and ready to fall apart any time. In fact, there were small bits of bones and a few fallen shoes on the ground. Most skeletons still retain their dry, peeling skin and the hair on the skull.

Each of the deceased is still dressed up in the same fashion clothes he/she was buried with centuries ago. They wear suits, long dresses, fur hats, bonnets, military uniforms, etc. Many are still dressed in their Sunday best. In an open coffin, a bishop can be seen with all his pontifical ornaments. Priests and monks still have their clerical vestments.

The last body to be placed in the Capuchin Catacombs was that of a girl called *Rosalia Lombardo*. She was two-years-old when she died in 1920. The girl's body is displayed in a glass coffin. She wears a long brownish dress and a yellow ribbon in her blond hair. Many people claim that her eyes blink at the day light. We observed her face: she looks as if she is sleeping. In fact, she has been nicknamed "The Sleeping Beauty of the Capuchin Catacombs".

Those Catacombs represent a museum of death, a place where the living people meet the dead. Moreover, the actual clothes they wore centuries ago provide a unique documentation of the fashion during the 16th, 17th, and 18th centuries. The view of those 8,000 bodies without souls was something touching. It left us with a lot to think about and made us appreciate life. Nobody felt like saying anything when we came out of that macabre place.

Although we ended our day with that ghostly experience, at Fiesta Hotel we enjoyed another pleasant evening. After dinner some of us went to the hotel's open-air theater in the garden. Others sat on the terrace, had a drink, and danced at the sound of an accordion. Rosario, a tourist from north Italy, was sitting alone in a table; he kept on looking at our Kelly and then he invited her to dance. She accepted with pleasure and the two danced till late under the bright moonlight.

Chapter 5

MAJESTIC SEGESTA, MEDIEVAL ERICE, UNLUCKY SELINUNTE

The program for day five of our Sicilian adventure called for a visit to the western part of the island. That morning my vacationers were well rested and impatient to go on that new discovery. The sky was blue, the sun brilliant, and the air fresh.

We took the freeway that goes from Palermo to Trapani. We drove by the airport and the blue sea on the right and a craggy mountain with the towns of Capaci, Carini, Cinisi on the left. Soon the wide plain of Partinico and Alcamo, covered with lush vineyards and olive trees, welcomed us. We left the freeway at the *Segesta Exit*, took a country road, and climbed a hill covered with wattles, wild flowers, thistles, and red poppies.

Roger was an attentive passenger, and, as we made a sharp turn, he started to wonder if he was hallucinating. "Holy macaroni", he said, "I am not sure, but I think I just saw an old temple up there. Are we in Greece?" It was a short-lived image, but not hallucination. He had just seen the famous *Temple of Segesta*.

We know that some 2,800 years ago, the Greeks invaded Sicilia Bedda and owned it for about 600 years. Think of the great progress made in America from the time of its discovery to our days. That has been only a period of time of about 500 years. Likewise, the Greeks had 600 years to transform Sicily into a very prosperous land with new cities and lasting monuments. Over time wars and earthquakes destroyed most cities, but many temples and ruins are still standing as witnesses of the glory that Greece was. The Temple of Segesta is one of them.

Some 2,500 years ago, on top of an idyllic hill, there was a prosperous Greek city called *Segesta*. In the 5th century B.C. it reached the peak of its economic and military power. Alas, sacked and plundered by the Vandals and the Arabs about 1,000 years ago, the city fell into total oblivion. Today, only ruins remain as evidence of its glorious past. Those silent ruins are found among agaves, prickly pears, thistles, cypress, and reddish rocks.

However, alone, on a hilltop with an impressive view of the surrounding countryside, Segesta's magic Doric Temple stands untouched. It is the most enchanting and captivating Greek temple in Sicily. It looks as if it was built yesterday and not 2,500 years ago! It is colossal, measuring 60-meters long and 26 wide. There are 14 columns on each side and 6 across the front and back. It could accommodate 4,000 people. Time and weather gave those columns a lovely golden color, which even today radiates light on a sunny day. Standing before it, "breathtaking" is the word that comes to mind. That solitary temple is surrounded by mystery, because for some unknown reason, it was never finished and never had a roof; the blue sky has always been its roof. Today, it is considered as a wonder of the ancient world, as history preserved and as a magic window open into the glorious Greek times. We took some time to admire that wonder and meditate on its brilliant life. We felt as if we were in ancient Greece. Yes, that temple has inspired generations of travelers and artists and it charmed us too.

A steep walk from the temple took us to another of Segesta's past glory, its open-air *Greek Amphitheater*, partially excavated into a rocky hillside, on top of a stunning mountain plateau with wonderful countryside views. The amphitheater could accommodate 4,000 spectators. The acoustics from the focal point are as good now as they were so many centuries ago. Today, during the summer months, that theater is used for Greek plays, dramas, concerts, and other events. The same hilltop contains also a few crumbling ruins of a Norman castle, a small Christian church and a mosque.

TEMPLE OF SEGESTA

At 11:00 a.m., we regrouped and continued on the freeway to Trapani, a charming city by the sea. Then, we proceeded towards *Erice*, a magnificent medieval town perched on top of San Giuliano Mountain, 2,500-feet above the sea level. A long and winding road took us up there. Our driver Giuseppe honked any time he made a sharp turn.

When we passed through a wooded area, Sandra asked, "Remo, what kind of animals live in this wood?" "Lions, tigers, bears", I answered with a grin. Immediately, everybody roared, "Lions, tigers, bears. Oh, my!" Are we going to see the Wizard of Oz?

Till then I had humorously called our bus driver "Corporal Giuseppe", but, because of his professional services and safe driving over the narrow and winding road to Erice, my cheerful people promoted him to "Captain Giuseppe".

While visiting the ruins of Segesta, we could only imagine what an illustrious city it must have been, in Erice we did not have to imagine, because we saw, touched, and walked through an ancient city that has fully kept its medieval aspect. The town has about 30,000 inhabitants.

We entered Erice through Porta Trapani (Trapani Gate), and from there, we walked on the neat street called Via Vittorio Emanuele. Soon we encountered Chiesa Matrice, a church built in 1314 with material taken from the ancient Temple of Venus. Then we wandered through narrow medieval streets, alleys, old houses,

35

churches, and courtyards. The streets were paved with large and glossy dark stones arranged in geometric patterns. Those stones had been polished by centuries of foot traffic. Some buildings had Arabic portals and decorations. Everything was old, but very clean. Walking through that maze of silent streets, it seemed that we were transported back in time to a medieval, fairy-tale town lost above the clouds.

At a certain point, we came to the front of the old Pepoli Norman Castle. Some of us went up to the terrace, and, Mamma Mia, what a magnificent panoramic view we had! Down below we could see the city of Trapani, small towns, the green countryside with valleys, plains, mountains, sandy beaches, San Vito lo Capo, the blue Mediterranean Sea and the Egadi Islands! It was breathtaking!

Finally, when we reached Piazza Umberto, the city's main square, we saw many quaint souvenir boutiques, snack bars, pastry shops, ice cream parlors, old bakeries, cafes, and small restaurants. We stopped at a restaurant with outside tables and ate local specialties. In particular we loved the popular "couscous", a traditional Arabic dish made of steamed balls of crushed durum wheat with semolina served with a stew. When Susan spotted a romantic couple holding hands in a nearby cafe, she sighed, "Oh, how I wish my Luigi was here with me!"

The sky had been clear and the air rather cool. Suddenly, at about 1:00 p.m., a thick fog came from the valley below and enveloped the entire town. The temperature dropped considerably. Luckily we had a light sweater. The fog gave us a good reason to get back to our bus.

Because of the charm of its medieval buildings and the spectacular panoramic views today, Erice has become a major tourist attraction; it is the destination of many intellectuals, daydreamers, and honeymooners. Yes, Erice won our heart too!

MEDIEVAL ERICE

Next, we descended down to the plain, bypassed the city of Trapani, drove by its white mounds of *Salt Pans*, and made a stop at *Donnafugata Winery* near the city of *Marsala*. Although it was not time to harvest the grapes and make wine, the owner showed us his vineyard and the huge wine cellar. He gave us a thorough explanation of the wine making process. His machinery was modern and impressive. Then he served us a generous dish of bread with olive oil, salami, cheese, prosciutto, olives, potato chips, cannoli, and peeled prickly pears. We tasted five kinds of wine: Sicily's famous sweet *Marsala* wine, the traditional *Cataratto Bianco*, the dessert *Moscato*, the fortified wine *Zibibbo*, and the sweet fortified *Cribari*. We took a lot of pictures and bought a few bottles of wine. When we left Donnafugata several people were laughing and singing; well, that was expected after five glasses of wine!

WINERY

On the road again, and in about 45 minutes, we arrived to *Selinunte* for a short visit. Located half way between Trapani and Agrigento, Selinunte was an ancient Greek city sitting on a high plateau overlooking the Mediterranean Sea. The name Selinunte derived from the quantity of wild parsley that grows in that area. The city was founded in 628 B.C., and within a short period of time, it became wealthy and powerful. Soon it embellished itself with public

37

markets, fortified walls, an active port, and eight splendid temples. Imagine, its largest temple was 370-feet long, 177 wide, and 100 high!

During that time, cities were kind of independent *City States* and were often at war with other cities. It happened that for some political reason, the neighboring Segesta, being at war with Selinunte, asked for help from the *Carthaginians* who lived on the northern shore of Africa. Those Africans had always attempted to set foot in Sicily and thus they gladly accepted to help. They came to Selinunte with an army of 100,000 men and laid siege to the town for 9 days. With incredible violence, they massacred 16,000 inhabitants, took 7,000 as slaves, and destroyed the entire city. Only a few people managed to escape.

In 409 B.C., Selinunte went overnight from being one of the most prominent Sicilian cities to a city of ruins, where only a few temples survived. Later, a powerful earthquake further reduced that once glorious city to a pile of rubbles. Since then Selinunte laid abandoned and its name fell into oblivion. Whatever was left remained buried under a layer of thick vegetation and an accumulation of sand carried by the Mediterranean winds.

Only some 2,400 years later, in the early 19th century, the work of excavation began. Today, the ruins brought back to light constitute the largest and most impressive archeological site in the Mediterranean. Visitors are astounded by the immense stretch of gigantic remains; among them are noticeable the ruins of five large temples, bits and pieces of the old protective walls, pieces of the fallen Acropolis, and the foundations of a market place.

Today, Selinunte is a real *mecca* for lovers of archeology and history. We were not archeologists, but we walked through those ruins and had an idea of what the splendor of that city must have been 2,400 years ago. We felt sad thinking of the carnage that took place there. It seemed that we were there right after the destruction of the city.

SELINUNTE

On the way back, we took a short cut through a country road. Something strange caught our attention: scattered along the road and in the middle of olive groves, we saw many gigantic and eroded cylindrical column-drum blocks, entirely cut from the bedrock and ready to be transported to Selinunte for the construction of temples. Numerous other large drums and capitals, partially broken, were seen among tall cactuses and weeds. They looked like abandoned toys of giant children.

Then, we passed by an ancient stone quarry called *Cave di Cusa* (Cusa Quarry), where all that material had been extracted. Looking at the walls of the quarry, we could see the round holes where the cylindrical drums had been hacked out and removed. We saw enormous blocks in various stages of carving lying on the ground; a few half-cut column sections were still attached to the mother stone, other sections were strewn amongst the grass or in the surrounding olive orchards, waiting to be transported. Some sections were marked out with a circle indicating the cylindrical area to be cut. We saw even the cave where the stone-cutters stored their tools.

The entire sight of the Cusa Quarry was mysterious, almost eerie. It seemed that the people who worked in there had just downed their tools and gone for lunch or on strike. They left everything abandoned; in reality their lunch-time or strike has lasted 2,400 years!

Why? Alas, because of the cruel war between Selinunte and the ruthless Carthaginians, all laborers in the quarry, fled the scene and escaped to safety. Consequently, all blocks of stone that were currently being worked on, were completely abandoned in the same state and place we see them today. The sight of those abandoned stones was for us more moving than the ruined temples themselves.

Thanks to the many column sections that still pepper the Cusa Quarry, we had a tangible idea of how the craftsmen and engineers extracted them. First, they marked on the limestone a circle about two-meters in diameter, indicating the circumference of the drum to be extracted. Then, the stone-cutters began chipping an opening around the circumference of about 50-inches, where they could stand while cutting the drum. Next, the workers chiseled the limestone until they reached a depth of about ten-feet and made a perfect limestone cylinder. After that, using metal tools, the base of the cylinder was chipped away until it could be levered from the mother stone underneath. Finally, the extracted material was placed on wooden wheels and

oxen pulled them to the construction site, where the drums were further polished and hoisted into position. Our visit to Cave di Cusa was a poignant
and educational experience; it seemed we were traveling through a factory
of temples!

CUSA: ABANDONED COLUMNS

Chapter 6

GOING ON A SENTIMENTAL JOURNEY

In the morning of day six of our tour, just as the sun peaked over the Tyrrhenian Sea, Angela came to the breakfast room singing, "I am going to take a sentimental journey…!" Paul echoed "This is the day the Lord has made. Alleluia!" They were so happy because their dream was about to come true; they were going to see the town their family roots.

Although the Italian explorer Cristoforo Colombo (Christopher Columbus) discovered America in 1492, it wasn't until early 1900s that a large number of Sicilians came to America. They left behind parents, brothers, sisters, friends, and affections. They were young, hard-working, and determined to build a better future in the land of opportunities. As time passed, most of them never had the opportunity of returning to Sicily. Then, as their children learned English, the Sicilian language became more and more a foreign language, and later all contacts with the *old country* went lost. However, the children and grandchildren of those emigrants always kept in their heart the desire of visiting the dear little town where their grandparents came from; they always wished to see the old house where they lived, to walk on the same roads they walked, to look at the same mountains, to eat the same food, and to meet their living relatives. Today, with the improved economy and faster ways of traveling, many *Sicilian-Americans* are making that dream come true.

In the past few days, we enjoyed seeing places known for their artistic works of art and archeological sites. There was nothing of that on day six of our tour, when we went to *Valledolmo and Contessa Entellina*, two small towns in the province of Palermo. Yet, that was a great day for my vacationers with Sicilian roots; in fact it was a great day for the entire group, because everybody enjoyed discovering life in country towns.

It was a beautiful sunny day with a temperature in the high 70s. At 8:30 a.m., we took the freeway towards Catania. Fifteen minutes later we exited by the village of Scillato, and, following the signs for *Valledolmo*, we drove up the hills on a narrow and winding country road. It was quite a challenging job for our *Captain Giuseppe:* although few cars were on the road, he had to proceed slowly and carefully, because there were small landslides, cracked pavement, fallen rocks, and some cattle crossing. Wild cactuses and a few palm trees bordered the road. The hills were covered with golden wheat, red poppies, and yellow mustard. A few farm houses were seen here and there. On the faraway horizon, the mountains had some snow on the highest peaks.

When we passed through the old town of Caltavuturo, we had to stop the bus, because a funeral procession was coming our way. It was preceded by a priest and a band playing funeral music. Following the band, four men carried a casket on their shoulders. A few people, dressed in black, walked right behind the casket; they were sobbing. A large crowd followed them. The women were reciting the rosary and the men walking silently. All of them looked at us with curiosity. Tour busses were a rare sight in that remote village. As we drove by the cemetery, we saw a large inscription above the gate "Qui per sempre riposano affetti, vanita', speranze" (Here forever rest affections, vanity, hopes).

Once we passed Caltavuturo, the road climbed up and the landscape became odd. The fields were completely void of trees, except along the streams down in the valleys. In the distant meadows, we saw white cows that some of us believed were rocks. A few huge and craggy stones, rising in the middle of the green fields, looked like giant teeth. Eagles and crows were landing on them.

That idyllic scene reminded me to tell the following story. "A farmer stands by a river bank with a wolf, a lamb, and a cabbage. He must take them safely across the river, one by one. Which one should he take first?"

"The wolf," Tony said.

"No, because then the lamb will eat the cabbage."

"The cabbage," Betty said.

"No, the wolf will eat the lamb."

"The lamb," Luigi shouted.

"You are right, because the wolf cannot eat the cabbage. What should he take next?"

"The lamb," answered Peter.

"No. The lamb will eat the cabbage, while the farmer goes back to get the wolf."

No one could give the right solution. I explained: first, the farmer should carry the lamb across the river; then he should carry the cabbage and take the lamb back. Next, he should take the wolf and finally go back for the lamb. Problem solved! Lupus in fabula! (speaking of the wolf!), while we were solving that farmer's problem, Captain Giuseppe had to stop the bus to let a large flock of sheep cross the road.

Finally, we reached Pizzo Sampieri, about 4,500 feet high. At the top, there were many wind mills for electricity production. "Eccolo!" (There it is!), I shouted. Down there, in a wide valley, I saw the town of Valledolmo like a mirage. Everybody rejoiced. We stopped the bus by the road sign "Benvenuti a Valledolmo" (Welcome to Valledolmo) and people with family roots in there had their picture taken by the sign. "Now I can prove to my *cumpari* (friends) back home that I have been here!" said Paul. Then, we crossed a small bridge and entered the town.

Valledolmo (Valley of Elms) is a medieval town of about 5,000 people; it lies at an altitude of 2,600 feet. Walking through Corso Garibaldi, the town's main street, we noticed that all side streets on the left go downhill and all streets on the right go uphill. It is impossible to drive or park a car on those steep, narrow, and old side streets. A small stone ramp provides access to most dwellings. There was a woman hanging white sheets on a cloth line attached to her neighbor's window. Two other women with a basket of groceries were walking with difficulty on those steep streets. When we saw a man and a woman walking with a donkey laden with wood, Angela asked if she could take a picture. The man nodded yes, but the woman was embarrassed and hid behind the donkey.

Most people in Valledolmo are farmers; they go to the fields in the morning and return home in the evening. They cultivate wheat, corn, grapes, and the renowned *siccagno tomatoes*. They also raise cattle, horses, sheep, and funny goats with twisted horns. In the early 1900s, many people from Valledolmo moved to the Buffalo, New York area.

VALLEDOLMO: GOOD FRIDAY PROCESSION

Our bus dropped us off at Piazza Generale Cadorna. It was 11:00 a.m. There, we found a group of people anxiously waiting for relatives they had never met before. I had previously informed the mayor and the parish priest of our visit. Within minutes, Angela and Mary Battaglia were able to find some distant cousins; they hugged warmly and disappeared to a side street. I entrusted Linda and Roger Vallone to the care of my friend Salvatore Gullo. He spoke some English and helped them find relatives. I instructed the rest of the group to be free and to return to the Piazza at 12:30 p.m. They went to visit the church and the palace of Baron Cutilli; they took pictures of the narrow streets, browsed inside a couple of grocery stores, and spent time in a coffee shop, where they socialized with a few men enquiring about their relatives in Buffalo.

I remained with Frank and Nancy Ippolito. Frank's grandfather came from Valledolmo, but he was not sure he still had living relatives there. That was when I used my usual approach to find relatives. Sitting on a long bench under a palm tree, there were at least ten elder men chatting. They all wore a black Sicilian *coppola* (cap). They looked at us with curiosity, and, when they heard us speaking a foreign language, they suspected we were tourists or invaders.

Tourists or invaders? With the exception of a few emigrants, no tourists ever go to that most remote mountain town!

I approached the men and said, "Buon Giorno a voi tutti. (Good morning to all of you). This man is Frank Ippolito; he is American, but his grandfather Vincenzo came from here. Do you know any Ippolito in town?" Immediately one of those men replied with a smile, "I am Ippolito", but he could not connect with Frank. He kindly walked us to the house of *Orazio Ippolito* and called, "Orazio, questi sono americani; credo che sono parenti con te" (Orazio, these are Americans; I believe they are related to you). Orazio, a man in the 80s, came to the door; he was smoking an old curved pipe. For a few seconds, he remained pensive, then, he smiled and asked. "Did you know my late brother Calogero Ippolito in Fredonia, New York?"

"Yes! He was my father's cousin! So, you and my father are cousins! Oh, my God!" shouted Frank with a trembling voice. Orazio and Frank hugged each other for a long time; tears filled their eyes. Orazio invited us inside and called his wife Carmela, who ran to her bedroom and put on a long colorful apron. She hugged Frank and Nancy and began to fill the table with cookies, grapes, figs, and soft drinks. Orazio ran to the cellar and came back with two bottles of red wine, made with his grapes. Our hosts opened their home and their heart to us. I had little chance to taste those goodies, because Frank and Orazio kept on talking and I was busy translating everything they said.

Frank placed on the table many photos of the Ippolito family in America. Pointing out to each picture, he gave the name of every person and explained how they were related to him. Carmela searched through her bundle of pictures and found one showing Frank's grandfather and the young Orazio. The back of that picture read "Valledolmo 1927". There were so many pictures that I became confused as to who was who. Nancy gave Orazio a small Statue of Liberty as a token gift. Then they exchanged addresses, telephone numbers, and promised to keep the contact alive. Carmela insisted that we stay for lunch, but we had made reservations in a restaurant for the entire group. Frank invited Orazio and Carmela to lunch with us. They kindly declined, but then accepted. "I want to be a little longer with my cousin!" said Orazio.

Frank and Orazio talked for a long time about their family in Fredonia and in Valledolmo, then Frank expressed a desire to visit the town and the house where his grandfather lived as a young man. Orazio and Carmela walked us to a nearby old stone house.

"This is where all Ippolito people lived, including your Nonno (grandfather) Vincenzo," said Orazio. Frank kissed the wall of that house, took pictures, and shed a few tears. He removed a little stone from the wall and picked a carnation flower from a pot. "These are my most precious souvenirs," he said. I found very interesting when Frank asked, "Uncle Orazio, Sicily is such a beautiful place, why did my grandparents leave it?" "They left because they had an empty stomach", responded Orazio.

We walked to the town's main square and looked at a monument with the name of local soldiers who died during the last two world wars; two of them were Ippolito. Then, we entered the Immaculate Conception Church where Frank's grandparents were married in 1917. Frank said a little prayer and shed a tear there too. The parish priest, Padre Raffaele, came and gave us a brief history of the church. Then he made a copy of the birth and marriage certificates of Frank's grandparents. Nancy made a little donation in their memory.

At 12:30 p.m., we boarded our bus and drove to *Fontana Murata*, a country restaurant with plenty of palm, pine, elm, and carob trees. There was even a tiny family chapel. A large stable had cows, horses, sheep, ducks, rabbits, and chickens. We took a lot of pictures.

The owners of the restaurant, *Mrs. Donata Gioia*, treated us like kings and queens. We ate a delicious antipasto, two kinds of pasta, three kinds of meat, salad, prickly pears, desserts, and all red and white wine we wanted! Sicilian folklore music made everyone go wild; many of us danced. Then, Donata gave us a tour of her house, a 17th century mansion. We liked her dining and living room, both decorated with classy and antique furniture. We loved Fontana Murata where we had a festival of food and fun!

At 3:00 p.m., Orazio and Carmela hugged Frank and Nancy and left saying, "Che bella sorpresa! Grazie! Dio vi benedica" (What a wonderful surprise. Thank You! May God bless you). Frank was so moved that he could barely talk. Later, he told us, "Oh, my God! I cannot believe this! I must come back with my children. This is the highlight of my tour. In Valledolmo, I thought of the pain my grandparents felt when they left parents, relatives, and friends. I was overpowered by emotion. At the same time, I was overjoyed to see the place where they lived and to reunite with my relatives. I feel like I belong to Valledolmo."

AT FONTANA MURATA

Then we drove to the town of *Contessa Entellina*. The country road was much like the one we took to Valledolmo: narrow, twisted, deserted. The landscape was made of vast undulating hills with golden wheat and pastures. My people did not notice all that, because, overcome by the delicious food and wine, they fell asleep. However Joe Schiro', David Cuccia, Bob Lala, and Betty Provenzano, all with family roots in Contessa E., were unable to sleep: their dream too was about to come true.

As we approached the town of Contessa Entellina, I picked up the microphone and shouted, "Wake up, wake up!" The Schiro', Cuccia, Lala, and Provenzano had their picture taken by the town's sign, which read, "*Contessa Entellina. Centro Albanese. Benvenuti. Hore Arbereshe. Mire Se Na Erdhit*". When we saw the street signs also written in two languages, we wondered if we were still in Sicily. Yes, we were, and in particular, we had just entered a town inhabited by people of Albanian origin.

The town of Contessa Entellina lies on a high plain framed by Mt. Genuardo on one side and rolling hills with wheat, vineyards, and olive trees on the other sides. The town has about 3,000 residents whose ancestors left Albania to escape the atrocities of the occupying Muslim Turks, some 500 years ago. They are known as *Arbereshe* or *Albanian Settlers*. Today, those people are fully integrated into the Sicilian life and language, but they still retain their

47

Arbereshe language, traditions, culture, customs, costumes, food, and religion. Their priests are called *Papas* and conduct the religious liturgy in the Greek Orthodox rite and language. There are several Arbereshe towns in Sicily.

Over the past 500 years, very little has changed in Contessa E. Strolling through its streets and talking with the locals, one can almost relive their past. Although they were prosperous and happy in Sicily, in the late 19th century a great number of them moved to the USA, and in particular to New Orleans, Louisiana, where they still form a strong group of Arbereshe proud of their origin.

We parked our bus in a side street and walked in front of Maria Santissima della Favara Church. There, we found many elderly men sitting in front of a café'; most of them had a suit and a necktie. They were surprised to see us in their remote town.

Before I could greet them, Nicola Fucarino approached us and asked, "Are you from New Orleans? I have a brother there". When those men found out that we were Americans and some of us had family roots in Contessa E., they became very friendly and offered to help.

When I told them, the last name of my four *American-Arbereshe* people, those men immediately contacted several people in town. Miracle: within minutes my good four people embraced relatives they had never met before! Showing photos and birth certificates of their grandparents helped to make that miracle. I did not have to interpret for them, because a few locals were proud to show some knowledge of English. Three of my four people were even able to somehow communicate in the Arbereshe tongue and a fourth one was helped by an old, skinny, and bearded man who was proud to tell he had been a barber in New Orleans and knew everybody there.

Where did my four Arbereshe people go? What did they do? I am not sure, but later they told us they met relatives, exchanged information and addresses, saw the house where their folks lived, took pictures of relatives and places, walked on the same streets their ancestors walked, prayed in the church where they prayed, and, of course, tasted some Arbereshe food and wine.

In the meantime, the rest of us browsed downtown, took pictures, went into a grocery store, and an Arbereshe souvenir shop. Then we sat at a café and chatted with locals. The news of our presence in town spread very quickly, and in no time, about 20 people came to the square, anxiously asking about their relatives in New Orleans; they gave messages for them. Even *Papa Nicolas Cuccia*, the parish priest, joined us at the café. He took us inside his church and gave a brief history of the Arbereshe people. Papa posed for a group picture on the church steps.

At 6:30 p.m., my American-Arbereshe hugged their relatives and Papa Nicolas. Then we took the freeway and arrived to our Fiesta Hotel just on time for dinner. On the bus my four people could barely hold their tears in telling how warmly they were received by their newly found relatives. "If they knew we were going, the entire town would have been there to see us!" said Betty.

Yes, for those four people that day was the highlight of their entire tour of Sicily. For them that little town was the most beautiful places on Earth; the modest house where their folks lived was the nicest museum and their grandparents were the greatest artists!

Back at Fiesta Hotel, we enjoyed another memorable evening of good food and fun. When Linda saw Rosario and Kelly dancing together in the moonlight, she sighed, "Ah, amore, amore! (Ah, love, love!) She is a lucky woman!"

ARBERESHE COSTUMES

Chapter 7

AGRIGENTO: THE WONDERS OF AKRAGAS

In Segesta we admired a splendid Greek temple, and in Selinunte, we felt sorry for what happened to that glorious Greek city. In this chapter, we talk about several other Greek wonders, and later in Siracusa and Taormina, we will discover more Greek marvels. Yet, there are even more Greek surprises in Tindari, Solunto, and in other places of the Sunny Island. It seems that writing about Sicily's historic sites is the same as writing about the history and civilization of ancient Greece itself. The reality is that, during the time Sicily became adorned with many superb cities and monuments, Sicily was indeed part of Greece itself. It was known as *Magna Graecia* (Greater Greece). Its wealth of architecture and monuments is what today constitutes Sicily's proud heritage. That is the reason why so many travelers go there and that is why we too are going to Agrigento today.

In the morning of day 7 of our tour at Fiesta Hotel, we enjoyed another late breakfast. Then we loaded our baggage on the bus, thanked our kind hosts, took more pictures in the tropical garden, and drove on the freeway towards the ancient Greek city of *Akragas* (today's Agrigento). On the way, we looked at the hinterland landscape and found it very picturesque: there were rolling hills with blazing golden sheaves of wheat, idyllic pastures with grazing cattle, a few isolated farm houses, several towns on hilltops, and a few snowcapped mountain peaks on the horizon. The sky was blue and the sun shining. Everything looked magic. When we came close to the city of Agrigento, we caught a glimpse of its famous *Valley of the Temples*, where one can find a large amount of Greek temples.

It was lunch time, thus we went straight to *Villa Kephos*, a country restaurant surrounded by greenery with palm, olive, fig, pomegranate trees, and a wonderful view of the Valley of the Temples. The owner of the restaurant, *Salvatore*, had prepared tables under a large tent. Two other tour groups were already eating there. We sat down and were served an exquisite Sicilian antipasto. Then we had three different kinds of aromatic pizza cooked in a wood-burning oven. Each kind of pizza had a different and unique delicious taste. We ate all the pizza we wanted. Next, we had salad, fresh figs, grapes, peeled prickly pears, and all the red and white wine we wanted. As a surprise, Salvatore brought in three Sicilian men, dressed in local folkloric costumes; they sang for us and played guitar and tambourine. Everybody was thrilled and danced. We had a barrel of fun!

AT VILLA KEPHOS

At 2:00 p.m., my friend *Enzo* came to the restaurant and had some pizza and wine with us; I had hired him as guide. Jokingly, I used to call him *Lieutenant Colombo*, because of his resemblance to the American actor. Enzo took us to the entrance gate of the Valley of Temples and called our attention.

"Ladies and Gentlemen, welcome to my beautiful Agrigento, the city that does not know a day without sun. Actually, there are two cities called Agrigento: the new and the old. The new Agrigento is really not so new; it is about 1,200 years old. Look at it, there on top of that hill overlooking the sea. The old Agrigento was called *Akragas* and it lies buried under that vast valley in front of us. Look, today the valley is covered with green vegetation and olive and almond trees. What attracts a large number of tourists here is not the new Agrigento, but Akragas, and let me tell you why."

"The ancient city of Akragas was founded by the Greeks in 582 B.C. It was magnificently situated on this high ridge with a view of the Mediterranean Sea. It had massive protective walls and nine entrance gates. At its height, it had a population of 400,000 people. The city expanded rapidly and became one of the richest, most beautiful, and most powerful cities in the Mediterranean. It embellished itself with sumptuous temples and attracted a large number of artists, writers, and philosophers. Among them was the illustrious philosopher Empedocles. The famous Greek poet Pyndar called Akragas, 'The most beautiful city built by mortal men'"

"Unfortunately, Akragas' fame did not last long. In 406, it was besieged, sacked, and destroyed by the Carthaginians. Those barbarians plundered the city, set fire to the temples, and carried all works of art to Carthage, then, they occupied the devastated region until 210 B.C. Later, the Romans seized Sicily and used the ruins as a military stronghold. In 828 A.D., the Carthaginians (then called Arabs) invaded again and reconstructed the old city on the hilltop, where we can see it today with the name of Agrigento."

"The old Akragas remained abandoned. Over the many centuries, earth and thick vegetation covered its glorious remains, most of which still is under fields of olive, almond, carob, fig, cactuses, and pistachio trees in front of us. However, traces of the city's splendor can still be seen in the temples that survived the human savagery and the natural catastrophes. Those are the most important testimony of the great Greek culture and architecture. Here you can see and touch history. A walk through these ruins brings the visitor 2,500 years back in time!" Enzo showed us a gnarled olive tree about 1,000-years-old, called *The Olive of Juno*.

Then, we climbed a short dusty slope and came face to face with the *Temple of Juno* built on a rocky ridge. "Juno was the wife of Jupiter and goddess of marriage, newlyweds, fertility, and childbirth", Enzo explained. "People mainly came here to get married and to pray to the goddess, whose huge statue was in the center of the temple. All newlywed couples had to sacrifice a lamb to Juno. Particularly interesting was the wedding ceremony. The priest took the right hand of the bride and groom and placed them on top of each other. Then the groom tied a belt around the bride's waste and the guests showered them with wheat and pomegranate seeds to wish them many children. A few months later, the couple returned to the temple and the pregnant woman offered her belt to Juno, since it became too tight. This place was also a romantic sanctuary where wives, embittered with the conduct of their unfaithful husbands, came to tell their problems to the goddess."

"Look at the golden color of the columns; they seem to glow at the sun light. Look at that reddish wall, it reminds us that in 406 the Carthaginians set fire to this temple in an attempt to destroy it. Of its many beautiful columns, only 25 are still standing, the rest fell over the hill during a landslide."

Rita and Steve surprised us when they knelt down and pretended to renew their wedding vows. For the ceremony, Enzo provided white sheets and crowns of laurel. Then, Clara started telling Juno about her husband's infidelity. Next, Laura sighed, "Please, Juno, bring back my Marcello to me. I cannot live without him!" Juno paid no attention to Clara and Laura's prayers: she had heard that nonsense before.

RENEWING WEDDING VOWS

53

Next, we strolled on a wide paved walkway gently descending downhill. There, we saw almond trees with fresh fruit everywhere. We picked a few to snack on. The soil in the surrounding fields was of a reddish color and had large cactuses.

My enthusiast new 27 *archeologists* walked close to Enzo and asked many questions. Paul wanted to know what inspired people to build such magnificent temples, who were the architects and builders, how, 2,500 years ago, they could cut, transport, lift and assemble those huge blocks and build temples without the modern sophisticated machinery. Our guide explained that the Greeks built many temples because they were very religious. The names of the architects and builders are unknown; the quarry for the construction material was about a mile away, on the hill overlooking the temples. The blocks were simply cut with chisels and hammers, transported by horses and cows and then lifted with an ingenious system of pulleys, levers, and derrick cranes. A real herculean and challenging work!

Next, we visited the outstanding *Temple of Concord*, the Roman goddess of harmony. We marveled at its golden structure, size, design, and beauty. It has remained structurally intact for 2,500 years! In fact, it is one of the best preserved Greek temples. Its longevity is mostly due to the fact that in the 6th century the temple was consecrated as Christian church dedicated to St. Peter and St. Paul. Before consecrating it, they had to expel from the Temple Eber and Raps, two ferocious pagan demons. Enzo told us about the *Festival of Almonds in Bloom* that takes place there in February. "It is something spectacular", he said.

CONCORD TEMPLE AND CENTURIES OLD OLIVE TREE

Not far from the Temple of Concord, on the right side of the walkway, we found a *Christian Necropolis* of the 3rd century. It had many open and empty tombs dug in the limestone. Roger walked ahead of us and laid in one of them. When his wife saw him, she screamed in horror and surprise.

A little further down, we climbed a few steps and made a quick stop at the *Temple of Castor and Pollux*, the legendary twin children of Jupiter and Juno. Of that splendid temple, only 4 columns remain; they have become the symbol of Agrigento. Traces of some white stucco on those columns can still be seen. The other columns and walls of the temple lie on the ground in an enormous pile. Most of them still show two U-shaped grooves used for lifting them.

Finally, we came in front of an immense and chaotic area with huge blocks scattered on the ground. "Holy cow, what happened here?" said Mike. "This was the *Temple of Zeus*, the god of gods", said Enzo. "It was built to thank him for the victory over the Carthaginians. The construction began in 480 B.C., but was left unfinished because those barbarians invaded again in 409 and sacked it." Later, said temple was completely destroyed by a strong earthquake. If completed, it would have been the largest temple in the Greek and Roman world. It was as wide as a modern football field and as high as a ten-story building. Each column was over 55-feet high and 13-feet thick. The base of each column was the size of a modern living room. The fluted grooves were so large that a man could fit into each of them. Part of the front side of the temple was supported by 38 enormous stone statues called *Telamons*. In fact, one of them can be seen lying on the ground among the ruins."

"It is almost impossible to have a full image of this temple", said Enzo. For more than 2,000 years it has been nothing but a massive heap of huge broken stones scattered all around, as if there had been a powerful explosion. The temple was further disfigured when, in the 18th century, much of its best stonework was used to build the nearby Port Empedocle."

Pretending to be Zeus, Mario stood on a piece of broken column and requested us to bow to him. "Mighty Zeus, you are no good. You couldn't even protect your own house!" rebuked Paul.

I was surprised to see my *archeologists* sincerely interested in learning about those ancient Greek temples. They followed the guide like enthusiastic students and asked many questions. Some took note of everything he said.

At the end of the tour, Enzo asked us to sit for a few minutes on one of those stones and visualize what that temple looked like before crumbling into ruins. "If these stones could talk, each of them would have a story to tell about Akragas' fabulous times" he said. "Give the stones some life and let them tell you about the hundreds of men who cut them in the quarry, transported them across the fields, and assembled them in here. Let them tell you about the countless skillful artists who gave them life and beauty. Think also of the proud crowds that gathered here for happy celebrations. Finally, think of the terror and despair people experienced when they saw their magnificent city and these temples sacked, burned, and destroyed. It must have been terrifying! Yes, it is difficult to imagine that the pile of ruins on the ground was once one of the greatest temples in the world."

RUINS OF ZEUS' TEMPLE

At the end of the walking tour, Enzo said, "Ladies and Gentlemen, our visit to the Valley of Temples is over. I wish I could talk to you about my Akragas for two days instead of two hours. I greatly appreciate the interest you showed during this short time. And now, my Dear, I declare each of you *Honorary Citizen* of my beloved Agrigento. Grazie. Come back to see us."

A stroll in that huge Valley of Temples was an amazing experience. We actually walked in the same footsteps of the ancient Greeks and we learned how skilled they were and how hard they worked. Yes, we felt like if we had traveled 2,500 years back in time. It was a living history lesson and we loved it!

Next, we drove back to central hinterland Sicily. We bypassed Caltanisetta and Enna and visited the large and modern *Cerere Pasta Factory*, outside the town of Assoro, right off the Palermo-Catania freeway. That entire area is suitable for the cultivation of fine durum wheat, known as *Sicily's Gold*. The factory is owned and operated by the *Meritello* family.

We were welcomed by an employee who took us to the visitors' center, where we had to put on a white uniform, a bonnet, and a plastic over our shoes. Then came *Mr. Salvatore Meritello* and gave us a tour of the factory and explained how pasta is produced.

"When harvested", he said, "the wheat is taken to our mills to produce high quality semolina. Once the chaff from the grain is removed, the grooved rollers transform the semolina into flour. Mixed with pure water, the quality flour forms a blend known as gluten, a mesh of protein that binds the hydrated starch granules. After the kneading phase, the mesh becomes elastic dough and is pushed through steel rollers for extrusion in different pasta shapes. The process continues with the drying, ventilation, and cooling phases. Finally, the product is placed into elegant bags and sent to distributors all over the world."

Salvatore showed us the variety of pasta in *short* and *long* shapes. Among the short pasta, he pointed out *penne, fusilli, rigatoni, tortiglioni, gnocchetti, anelli siciliani, farfalle, gigli, and pipe.* Of those the most popular are the *penne and rigatoni*, so much used every day of the week. Among the long pasta shapes, Salvatore showed us *spaghetti, vermicelli, linguine, fettuccelle, stelline*, etc.

"All our pasta is produced with wheat grown under the warm Sicilian sun", he said. "At the table, the spaghetti cheerfully twine around the fork and make people happy all over the world."

We were impressed by the size, neatness, and magnificence of Cerere Factory. The machinery was modern, the employees, all dressed in white uniforms, were friendly and helpful. Salvatore was very knowledgeable about pasta making; we took a group picture with him. On our way out, we found a nice surprise: for each of us, he had prepared a bag with the inscription *Welcome to Cerere Pasta Factory*. Inside the bag, we found samples of its best products and some literature about the factory. "When you go back home, look for our pasta label in your grocery store," he said.

AT PASTA FACTORY

At 6:30 p.m., we checked into the deluxe Federico II Hotel, located just outside the city of Enna. The hotel was recently built; the rooms were neat and spacious with large beds, walk-in wardrobes, huge bathrooms, and a beautiful panoramic view of the countryside. At dinner we were treated like kings and queens. The waiters wore a black suit and white gloves. Food and wine were plenty and delicious. In an adjacent dining room, there was a private party; men had black suits and a ties and women wore beautiful long dresses. We could hear them dancing to the sounds of an accordion and a tambourine. We would have loved to join them, but we did not dare, because we were still in our casual attire.

Chapter 8

THE SURPRISE OF VILLA CASALE

The Hotel Frederic II was located in *Enna Bassa* (Lower Enna, modern part of the city), but everybody wanted to visit *Enna Alta* (Higher Enna), a medieval city perched on top of a nearly-inaccessible rocky plateau towering above the surrounding countryside, valleys, and towns. Because of its altitude of more than 3,000-feet above the sea level, Enna has earned the nickname of *The Belvedere of Sicily*. The city has about 75,000 inhabitants.

Early in the morning, we were awakened by a rooster crowing from a nearby farm. The sky was azure blue and there wasn't a cloud in sight. After a healthy breakfast, Captain Giuseppe drove to Enna Alta and dropped us by Café' Belvedere on Via Vulturo. It was truly a *belvedere*, because from there, we enjoyed a spectacular view of the entire countryside down below and a cool mountain air. We had some free time to stroll on Main Street and browse in a few stores. We tasted a delicious cappuccino and ate *cannoli, vinciatutti, fried cardi, and almond cookies*. At 12:00 noon we regrouped and took the road to Villa Casale, near the town of Piazza Armerina.

On the way, Mario asked, "Sometimes people tell me that I am and FBI and my wife is an IBM. That is funny. What does it mean?" "Yes, you are a Full Blood Italian and she is an Italian By Marriage". I explained.

Next, as we drove by a lake surrounded by verdant hills, I said, "Look at that lake on your left; it is *Lake Pergusa*. The ancient people believed that it was the entrance to the underworld where Pluto was the ruler. One day the young and beautiful *Proserpina* was picking flowers by that lake; *Pluto* saw her from his chariot, fell in love with her, and carried her away. The girl's mother *Ceres*, known as *Mother Nature* and patron of the harvest and fields' fertility, became so distressed that she neglected to take care of Earth's crops. Consequently, there was a great famine; people began to die of starvation. Jupiter summoned Pluto and Ceres and declared that Proserpina should stay six months with Pluto and six months with her mother. Ceres accepted the settlement and that gave birth to the four seasons. In spring and summer Ceres is happy with Proserpina, and thus, we have good weather and plenty of crops. In fall and winter Ceres is sad, mourns, and grieves, because of her daughter's absence; that is why we have bad weather and no crops."

"Mamma Ceres was a selfish mother", remarked Mary. "Didn't she know that pretty Proserpina would be married and leave her some day?" "Poor Pluto, he was a part-time husband!" echoed John.

PLUTO KIDNAPPING PROSERPINA

Soon after Lake Pergusa, we arrived at *Piazza Armerina*, a medieval town perched on top of a hill in central Sicily. A couple of miles away, there is an old Roman villa, called *Villa Casale*; actually, size wise it is more than a villa, it is a village. It was built around the year 350 A.D. and that means about 1,700 years ago. The Villa, an opulent Roman residence, was used as a summer hunting lodge. We don't know exactly who owned it; perhaps it was built for Maximian Herculius, a co-emperor with Diocletian.

After being inhabited for many centuries, the entire Villa and its precious mosaics and paintings were buried under a huge landslide. Time passed and the villa was entirely forgotten. Farmers cultivated crops on top of it. Finally, in 1950, it was rediscovered and excavations began. Surprise: the mud that covered the villa actually protected its mosaics and paintings.

In Palermo and in Monreale, we were amazed by the splendid Norman mosaic art works; in Villa Casale, we were equally stunned by the newly discovered mosaics and those are almost 1,000-years older than the ones we had seen the previous days. Moreover, to see the Norman mosaics, we had to look up to the walls and ceiling, but in Villa Casale, we had to look down, because all mosaic works are on the floor.

We found our local guide *Dino* waiting for us at the villa's entrance. We followed him with eagerness. He walked us on glass boardwalks suspended ten-feet above the mosaics. He stopped in each room and explained what we were seeing. It is impossible to describe here everything we saw. Dear Reader, if you can hold your breath for awhile, I give a short list.

We saw fabulous mosaics depicting mythological scenes, like the Cyclop Poliphemus receiving a cup of wine from Ulysses, Amore, and Psiche, the fight between Eros and Pan, Arion, Licurgus killing Ambrosia, Anphione's children playing and dancing, Hercules' labors, Hercules defeating the giants, Homeric poems, scenes of the Roman aristocracy daily life, erotic life, hunting parties, four-horse chariot races, horse riders, circus scenes, children playing, amorini, and cupids fishing, legends, battle scenes, fishermen, theater competitions, scenes of vines cultivation, picking and stumping grapes, multicolored mosaics in geometrical patterns, the four seasons, heads of wild animals, embarkation of animals, capture of rhinoceros, Emperor Maximian escorted by soldiers, ladies of the villa, fishing boats, and many more. Mamma Mia, what a surprise for art lovers!

The most surprising mosaic scene depicts *ten young women in bikinis* performing sports, including weight-lifting, discus throwing, running and playing with a colored ball. They are wearing the first bikinis in record. The Hall of the Great Hunt stretches over 150-feet and about 25-feet wide; it depicts the capture and transportation of wild animals destined for the spectacles held in the Roman amphitheaters. Particularly beautiful are the mosaics depicting a wounded lion attacking a hunter, the capture of a female tiger, young boys hunting a rabbit, and so on and so on.

The way those mosaics are perfectly conserved is astonishing. They are considered to be among the most beautiful and best-preserved mosaics and paintings anywhere in the world. They are astonishing, even for those who are not interested in history and arts. They are a fabulous window on the life of the privileged Romans about 1,700 years ago. Walking through those mosaic scenes, one feels like being in a movie theater.

VILLA CASALE: WOMEN IN BIKINIS

After Villa Casale, we drove by the town of Valguarnera and then through the Palermo-Catania freeway bordered by vast undulating hills, all covered with golden wheat. About 20 minutes later, we left the freeway and visited the neat and modern *Caseificio Gaetello* (Gaetello Cheese Factory) in the town of Ramacca. We were welcomed by a large flock of sheep grazing around the factory. First, they looked at us with suspicion, but when we started speaking their language, they all came to see us. However, just for precaution, they were escorted by two rams and a dog. Besides the smell of sheep, in the farm, there was a scent of orange and lemon trees in full bloom.

Then, the owner of the factory, Signora Maria Angela, came out and received us very warmly. She gave us a tour of her large plant and explained the entire process of cheese making. We saw a few men hanging on rafters large, yellowish rounds of cheese; others were draining cheese in reed baskets. Several women had their hands in a long tub; they were squeezing something white that looked like mozzarella. We stood around them, watched, and took pictures. In the show room, we saw so many kinds of cheese that we were unable to count them all. We were mostly impressed by the *provola cheese, fresh ricotta, fresh mozzarella, scamorzetta, and caciocavallo*. Of course, we tasted some of them with bread, olive oil, and delicious wine. Everything was so good, and Maria Angela so gracious!

GAETELLO CHEESE FACTORY

Next, we descended to the *Pianura di Catania* (Catania's Plain), the largest plain of Sicily, known for the fertility of its soil. That entire plain is covered with millions of orange and lemon trees. The fruit is exported all over Italy and Europe. When we reached the suburb of Catania, we took the freeway going south and checked into Hotel Panorama in Siracusa, where we stayed one night.

Chapter 9

A DAY IN GLORIOUS SIRACUSA

The city of Syracuse, New York, is named after the glorious *Siracusa*, a city in south-east Sicily. The two are separated by 6,000 miles and by some 2,700 years of history. Let's learn about the splendid heritage of the Sicilian city, so its American sister-city can be proud of that name.

Day nine of our memorable tour was another sunny and mild day. As I opened the window of my bedroom, a swarm of screeching swallows flew right in front of my eyes. They were intent on scooping up insects for their breakfast. While I was eating my breakfast, Clara came down signing. "Oh, what a beautiful morning. Oh, what a beautiful day. Yes, everything is going my way… " Clara was happy because she was going to Brucoli, a small town north of Siracusa. I arranged for Antonino, a local gentleman who spoke a broken English, to take her to Brucoli and help find her relatives. Antonino made all that possible and Clara's dream came true.

At 9:00 a.m., the rest of my enthusiast vacationers (26 now) were anxiously waiting to explore *Siracusa* and learn about its history. The city was built by the Greeks 2,700 years ago and soon became a great economic and military power. At a point in time, it competed with Athens itself for the dominion of the Mediterranean. The Roman writer Cicero described it as being "The greatest Greek city and the most beautiful of them all". Even today Siracusa presents itself as one of the best Greek-Sicilian cities to be visited. Here, one can discover the inner history of Sicily with Greek temples, churches, and castles. Nowadays the city counts about 150,000 inhabitants.

The city of Siracusa can be distinguished into three parts: the *Modern*, the *Historical* (known as Ortigia), and the *Archeologic*. The modern part is of no interest for tourists. Later, our guide Silvestro will tell us all about the *Archaeologic* section. Now let's discover *Ortigia*.

Our Captain Giuseppe dropped us off at the entrance of *Ortigia*, a small island connected to mainland Sicily by two bridges. That is where the first Greeks settled 2,700 years ago. Because it has been inhabited since then, one would expect to find there old buildings and caverns, but it is not so. The place has much changed over the course of centuries.

As we walked through the wide and neat *Corso Giacomo Matteotti*, we were surprised to see the place lined with splendid baroque palaces, churches, and historic buildings, all dating from the 17th and 18th centuries. There were elegant shops, restaurants, sidewalk cafes, bars, clubs, and busy local people. A few horse-drawn carriages were carrying cheerful tourists.

When we arrived to Piazza Duomo, we took a coffee break and watched people go by. A few of us visited the monumental baroque church of *Santa Lucia* (St. Lucy), which initially was a Greek temple dedicated to Athena, goddess of Wisdom. Inside the church, we admired remains of said temple and the large painting of the *Burial of Saint Lucy* by the famous painter Caravaggio.

Then we wandered aimlessly through a maze of medieval and quaint narrow streets, alleys, squares, and a large fruit market. We found a surprise at every corner. We passed by the remains of the Temple of Apollo and a large fish and fruit market.

Suddenly, we arrived to the beautiful *Lungomare* (Boardwalk), where we enjoyed an amazing view of the deep-blue Ionian Sea and discovered the soul of the city with quaint cafes crowded with tourists savoring Sicilian delicacies and watching the world go by.

Further down on the Lungomare, we saw a group of tourists standing by a high wall and taking pictures of something in a small and circular pond. The wall separated the pond from the waters of the sea. We stopped and heard a tourist guide say, "Ladies and Gentlemen, this is the famous *Fountain of Arethusa*. Look at the ducks, fish, and papyrus reeds in it. Now look carefully: can you see that clear water-spring gushing right in the middle of the pond? That spring is the *Nymph Arethusa* in person!

That fountain has inspired many poets and writers. The Greek poet Pindar, said that guide, tells us a charming legend about Arethusa. One day, while Arethusa was bathing in a mountain river of Arcadia, Greece, the god of that river, *Alpheus*, saw her and fell madly in love with her. The Nymph didn't share his feeling and ran away, but Alpheus chased her. To escape from him, she transformed herself into a stream of water, traveled under the Mediterranean Sea, and returned to the surface right in the center of this pond. In fact, they say that if you toss a goblet into the same river in Arcadia, it will pop up right here. Alpheus did not give up; he transformed himself into a stream of water, met up with Arethusa, intertwined with her water, and the two lived together ever since." Luisa sighed, "What a fascinating love story!" But Tony chastised her, "Oh, please, Luisa, don't make me laugh!"

I gave my 26 new *Siracusani* two hours of free time to walk around, shop, and have lunch. "Be back here at 2:00 p.m. in front of this nice Luna Rossa Restaurant", I instructed. Roger and Susan remained a little longer by the pond; they seemed to be day-dreaming.

SIRACUSA-ORTIGIA: BOARDWALK

At 2:00 p.m., everyone returned cheerfully and laughing. I could clearly see that they had good time and good wine. Captain Giuseppe arrived and drove us to the *Archaeological* section of Siracusa. There we met our guide *Silvestro*, a slender man in his 60s with whitish hair and a short beard. He greeted everybody. "Buon Giorno, Signore e Signori, and welcome to my beautiful Siracusa. We are standing on a very popular tourist place, because of its history and archeological sites. Let me tell you about the glorious olden time of my city."

"Siracusa was founded in 734 B.C. by Greek settlers. First, they inhabited the isle of Ortigia and then expanded to the mainland. Later, with a population of more than 250,000 people, it became a great economic and military power in the entire Mediterranean Sea. In the 5th century, the city rivaled with Athens itself. Its royal court was filled with famous men, like the great mathematician Archimedes, the illustrious playwrights Aeschylus, Euripides, and Pyndar. The philosopher Plato lived here for a long time."

"That splendid civilization and power caused conflict with another super-power in the Mediterranean, the Carthaginians. In 480, Siracusa defeated them at the Himera battle and took thousands of prisoners. In 414, it won a war against Athens. After that, for 200 years, the city enjoyed peace, prospered even more, embellished itself with temples, amphitheater, and many splendid public buildings."

"Unfortunately, in 214 B.C., Siracusa capitulated to the Romans. We know that during the war, Archimedes used his famous parabolic *ustor mirrors*, which focused the sun rays to set the enemy ships on fire. However, that did not save the city's independence. Under the Roman domination, Siracusa lost forever its power, and much later, it came under the control of the Barbarians, Arabs, Normans, Swabians, Byzantines, Spaniards, Bourbons, and finally the Italians. Today, Siracusa lives of its glorious past. Now let us see and touch a few remains of that past splendor." Silvestro walked us to a massive pile of ruins.

Since we were wondering what that could be, he explained, "This is the *Altar of Hieron*, built in 225 B.C. It was dedicated to Zeus Eleutherios, the god of freedom. Being 600-feet long and 60-feet wide, it was the largest altar known in the ancient world. As you can see, of it only the foundation has survived. The Altar was used mostly to celebrate the Eleutheria Festivals and other festivities in honor of the almighty Zeus. The historian Diodorus wrote that on a special occasion 450 bulls were slaughtered and sacrificed simultaneous atop this altar during the annual feast of Zeus. Look, you can even see the long grooves used to drain the blood of that many animals."

Immediately Anna whined, "Silvestro, stop; I am going to be sick!" Some men grumbled: "Where did they get that many bulls? Can you imagine the grief of the widowed cows?"

From the Altar, we walked to the famous *Greek Amphitheater*, the largest amphitheater surviving in the world. Silvestro told us, "As you can see, this amphitheater has been cut directly from the bedrock. It was done in the 5th century B.C. Look at the size: it measures about 400-feet in diameter and has 67 rows of bleachers. Fifteen-thousand spectators could sit on them. What a masterpiece of human ingenuity!"

"This amphitheater was used to educate the ancient people through dramas, tragedies, music, and poetry. It was used also for meetings, popular assemblies, political platforms, and circus games. Euripides, Aeschylus, and Sophocles came here to perform their tragedies. Plato and Archimedes came here too. This amphitheater is a testament of the glorious Siracusa. Here you can see and touch history. Unfortunately, with the advent of the barbarian hordes, this magic place was abandoned, and later, most of its material was used to build fortifications and defense walls. Only what was carved into the rock has been left."

"Despite of its abandoned state, this Amphitheater remains one of the most beautiful places of the ancient world. Today, during the tourist season, the glories of the Greek dramas, tragedies, epic myths, and legends are still performed here. Every year thousands of enthusiastic tourists from all over the world come to attend classic plays."

We did not visit the main stage, because several people, dressed in funny clothes, were rehearsing the Antigone of Sophocles. Silvestro walked us close to the top bleachers from where we had an excellent view of the entire place.

On a small rock overlooking the Amphitheater, there is a little two-story house with two windows; it looks like a tower. Tony tried to make us believe that he saw the ghost of the 2,200-year-old and famous Archimedes looking at our women. Tony insisted that the scientist was on the top window and had a powerful binocular. I think Tony was overcome by the magnitude of the place and by the history we were experiencing.

When Silvestro gave us some free time, a few of my cheerful *spectators* sat at the top of the amphitheater and dreamed. Later, Betty told us, "I closed my eyes, stepped back in time, and fantasized. I saw Greek actors play the *Aga-memnon* of Aeschylus. I saw the amphitheater filled with ancient people in their togas watching that famous tragedy. I could actually hear the shouting and the outbursts of the spectators! Wow, I could see and touch history! What an emotional feeling! What a daydream I had!"

SIRACUSA: GREEK AMPHITHEATER

Next, Silvestro took us to see a *Latomia*, which is a large limestone quarry from where the stones for construction of the ancient Siracusa and its monuments were extracted. The huge cavity we see today in the quarry was hewn out of hard rock and is about 100-feet below the ground level. Erosion, cave-ins, and high humidity have transformed that entire quarry into a large cave filled with lush vegetation of orange and lemon trees. The most renowned part of that Latomia is known as *The Ear of Dionysius*, so called because of its similarity to the human ear.

Silvestro explained, "This part of the quarry, the one that looks like an ear, is 23-meters high. It is known for its perfect acoustic quality, which amplifies by as much as 16 times, even the softest sounds, as they bounce off the walls. History says that in 414 B.C., *Dionysius*, the absolute ruler of Siracusa, kept in that cave 7,000 war prisoners and allowed them to die of disease and starvation. Legend also tells that from an opening above the *Ear*, Dionysius used to listen to the plans and secrets of those prisoners, even when they were just whispering."

Because of that awful story, as we descended into the Ear, we felt as if we were entering a spooky place. Moreover, there were birds that, with their shrieks, gave us goose bumps. Mario and Mary were walking ahead of us. Testing the Ear's acoustic, Frank whispered, "Mario, did you ever cheat on your wife?" Immediately Mario responded, "No, I did not". Then he looked around, but there was nobody near him. "Who said that?" Mario asked. "I am Dionysius, I know what you did", thundered Frank with a croaky voice!

SIRACUSA: THE EAR OF DIONYSIUS

During the walking tour, we noticed that Silvestro kept on looking at Evelyn and directing his attention mostly to her, as if she was the only person in the group. Evelyn felt flattered and invited him to have dinner with us. He gladly accepted, and, obviously, the two sat next to each other. Later, a few men in the group teased Evelyn and referred to Silvestro as her *boyfriend*!

Several people in the group expressed a desire to visit the church of the *Crying Madonna*, therefore we made a quick stop there. They say that in the morning of August 29th, 1959 in a private house in Siracusa, a little statue, representing the Virgin Mary, began to shed tears. The phenomenon was repeated four more days. The tears were collected and analyzed by reputable experts and were declared to be true human tears. A large church was then built to accommodate the number of pilgrims going there.

Besides being a magic place of sun, beaches, and historic ruins, Sicily is also famous for its delicious citrus products. In particular, the area between Siracusa and Catania is known for its vast groves of red oranges, such as the *blood oranges, sanguinello, tarocco, and moro.* Today, blood oranges are considered the hallmark of the Sicilian citrus.

During the previous days in Sunny Island, often we passed by orange groves, but we never stopped to see them closely. We decided that we should not end our tour without having that pleasure. Therefore, on our way from Siracusa to our next hotel, we made a detour and went to visit *Il Biviere*, a farm in the town of Lentini. The farm has at least 500 acres cultivated with red oranges and lemons. The private road to the farm is bordered with almond trees and tall cactuses. Behind them we could see long rows of trees loaded with golden oranges hanging from the branches or peaking between green leaves. The air we breathed had a scent of pleasant perfume. Way beyond the orange groves, there was an impressive view of Mt. Etna with snow and smoke on top.

The Biviere's family dog welcomed us with a waggling tail. Then the owner, *Signor Borghese*, shook everybody's hand and walked us to his groves, where a few men in blue overalls were picking oranges. We touched the golden fruit and took pictures. Then, Mr. Borghese took us inside the building equipped with modern machinery. There we found several men and women, all in green uniforms, working in the production, canning, packing, and shipping area. Our host gave a thorough explanation of everything we saw.

Next, we visited the shop filled with jars of orange products, including honey and marmalades. *Mrs. Borghese* came and served us delicious slices of different kinds of oranges, a few peeled prickly pears, and sweet orange juices. In particular we loved the *blood orange* that looked as red as fire. A glass of *sanguinello orange juice* sweetened our mouth until the evening dinner. The visit at Il Biviere was a unique experience. Besides enjoying a variety of the orange products, we were enchanted by the warm hospitality of our hosts and by the beauty of their farm. It was a pleasant walk in nature!

BLOOD ORANGE

At 5:00 p.m., we boarded our bus and drove north. When we passed by the city of Catania, we saw the most spectacular scene in the entire Sunny Island: Mt. Etna had fresh snow on its highest peak and black smoke coming out of the crater. We will talk about Etna in another chapter.

Finally, we arrived to our Hotel Antares, suspended on a hillside with a stunning view of the deep blue Ionian Sea. Each of us had a room with a balcony overlooking the sea. We stayed in that hotel three days. After dinner we relaxed on a large terrace with dancing music. There was a group of tourists from Spain; they danced like professionals. We mingled with them and learned some Latino dances. Later that evening, we wished everybody *Buenas Noches, Buona Notte, Good Night.*

Chapter 10

TAORMINA THE BEAUTIFUL

Sicily is known as the land of sun, deep-blue sea, mild weather, pristine beaches, spectacular scenery, famous historic sites, good food, and friendly people. However, one cannot expect to find all of these qualities in every corner of the Sunny Island. Yet, there is one place where visitors can certainly find them all; that place is Taormina!

Of all the gifts that Mother Nature has endowed Taormina, the most spectacular ones are its stunning panoramic view of the blue Ionian Sea and the majestic Mt. Etna puffing smoke and fire on the horizon. It is a splendor of the nature, a unique sight on Earth.

Spectacularly perched on the side of a mountain, *Taormina* is a legendary resort town that has the perfect mix of Sicilian spirit and glamour. It is the pearl of the Ionian Sea and a very popular tourist destination. Its natural beauty enchants and seduces the eyes, the mind, and the imagination. As soon as one arrives downtown, he/she feels the magical atmosphere of the place. Painters, poets, artists, philosophers, honeymooners, and travelers have fallen in love with it since the oldest times. When we think of Taormina, *Bella* (Beautiful) is the only word that actually comes to mind. The German writer J.W. Goethe defined it as "A piece of paradise on earth". People from all over the world flock there to enjoy that spectacular view, to stroll along its well-preserved medieval streets, and to have a taste of the Sicilian *Dolce*

Vita (Sweet Life). The town has about 15,000 inhabitants and relies heavily on tourism.

In the morning of day ten of our tour, while I was watching the sunrise over the Ionian Sea, I heard Luigi sing, "When the sun hits your eyes like a big pizza pie, you are in love…" Then, from another window, Betty echoed, "Volare, oh, oh. Cantare, oh, oh…." Yes, my lively people were more than ready to go to Taormina and have the time of their life. They were so excited also because that was the day they had been waiting for a shopping spree!

At breakfast a few ladies began to tease me, "Ah, ah, I saw you dancing with those Spanish women last night. Did you dream of them too? Are you married? Do you miss your wife? Do you have children? Are you going back home after this tour?"

I cut off that kind of enquiring and asked, "Ladies, do you know what *breakfast* means? It means you *broke* your *fast*. You fasted during the night and now you broke it. You did not fast too long."

At 9:00 a.m., we took a cable car from the shore, and 15 minutes later, we entered Taormina through Porta Messina (Messina Gate). My 27 new *Taorminesi* (inhabitants of Taormina) followed me like a troop of cheerful boyscouts. At *Piazza Vittorio Emanuele*, I stood on a bench and shouted, "Come closer." Mary and Betty ran by my side and began to sing Sinatra's song, "Fly me to the moon…"

I instructed, "Signore e Signori, we are now in the heart of famous Taormina. This is the free day you have been waiting for. Look at that crowded street in front of you; it is *Corso Umberto*, the town's main street with plenty of shops, cafes, and restaurants. It is about a mile long; at halfway you will find a charming square, called *Belvedere*. There you will find the most spectacular views of the sea and Mt. Etna. To your left, you can see the sign *Via Teatro Greco* (Greek Theater Street); it takes you to the famous 2,300-year-old Greek Theater. Make sure you see it; you will love it. Remember that this is your best and last chance to do your shopping. It is now ten o'clock; be back here at 5:00 p.m. Now go and enjoy your freedom!" Within seconds everybody disappeared among the crowd on Corso Umberto.

I remained alone and walked slowly. Surprise, there I saw Rosario; he asked about Kelly's whereabouts. Remember that they had met at Fiesta Hotel. I told him she might be somewhere shopping on that street. Later, I saw them walking together, hand in hand, just like Romeo and Juliet.

TAORMINA: GREEK THEATER AND MT. ETNA

At 5:00 p.m., everybody came back to Piazza Garibaldi. Like Christmas shoppers, many were carrying bags filled with souvenirs and expensive things that they were proud to show us. Ann whined, "I wish I could stay here a couple of more hours!"

At the hotel, there was no music after dinner; we sat on the large terrace with a magnificent night view of the town below. We drank wine, sang, and chatted till late. I asked for volunteers to tell what they had done during their free time in Taormina.

Immediately *Paul* said with an air of pride, "Betty and I walked not once but twice the length of lovely Corso Umberto. It is a very clean street with tables on sidewalks and colorful pots of flowers. There are many beautiful 15th and 16th century palaces, cafes, bars, restaurants, gelaterias (ice-cream parlors), cute boutiques that sell souvenirs, clothes, crafts, and ceramics. We visited an old church, peeked into a few stores, and did a lot of window shopping. We saw two wedding processions; one was coming out of St. Catherine Church and the other posing for pictures on the spectacular Piazza Belvedere. Then we sat down at an outside café, ate cannoli, enjoyed a cappuccino, and relaxed watching the world go by. There were many tourists relaxing in that café'; among them a woman with elegant clothes and a large pink hat caught my attention. Sitting on a small round table, she was feeding crumbs to a couple of birds and smiling to every gentleman passing by. I believe she was day-dreaming. Then, we went inside the Greek Theater and took a lot of pictures. Next, we had a delicious pizza and home-made wine at Mamma Rosa restaurant. After that we walked in a maze of narrow side streets and got a real feel of the local daily life. We felt like we were on a Hollywood movie. Oh, yes, believe me, a visit to Taormina means stroll, spend, eat, and drink. We loved it."

Frank wanted to share his adventure. "After some strolling and shopping along Corso Umberto, Nancy and I concentrated on the famous Greek Theater, the symbol and pride of Taormina. I was anxious to see and touch what I had seen in pictures. The theater was built on a sloping hill in the 3rd century B.C. It has 25 tiers of seats, all hewn out of a rocky slope, and they are all well preserved. It can accommodate 4,000 spectators. The Theater is still used in summer for events of international films, dances, festivals, concerts, fashion shows, and classic theatrical performances, including works of Aeschylus, Sophocles, Euripides, and Aristophanes. The glimmering waters of the blue Ionian Sea down below and the snow capped and smoking Mt. Etna make the most spectacular backdrop any theater could have. After a while, Nancy and I sat quietly on those stone steps and closed our eyes: we envisioned ourselves sitting with other spectators and marveled at what was going in there more than 2,000 years ago. It was a startling and humbling experience."

Roger volunteered to tell his story. "I wandered aimlessly through narrow and twisted medieval side streets like a lone star and then I ended up in the beautiful City Garden. It was a peaceful place away from the hustle and bustle of Corso Umberto. There was a bronze statue of a romantic young couple on a bench welcoming the visitors. That sets the feel for what to expect in the garden. There was a large amount of tropical plants, bougainvillea's, and rhododendrons in bloom, flower beds, lawns, edges, bushes, a pond with waterfall, huge parrot cages, and terraces with fabulous views on the countryside. There were also many statues, including that of Tsar Nicholas. Some people were sitting on benches and basking in the sun. It was a lovely place to relax, breathe, and meditate. Later, back on the street, as I saw a snack bar advertising *panini* (sandwiches), I sat down and had a *panino* with home-made bread, olive oil, raw prosciutto (ham), mozzarella cheese, and two glasses of red wine. I truly enjoyed my day."

Laura recounted, "Mary and I did a lot of window and real shopping and, when we got tired of walking, we sat on an outside café' at Piazza Belvedere.

We had a *tiramisu* and a delicious cappuccino. Piazza Belvedere is where many tourists hang out, stop for ice cream, drink a glass of wine, eat pizza, admire great views, watch street artists, and listen to street musicians. We love Taormina!"

TAORMINA: CORSO UMBERTO

"And you, *Mike*, what did you do?" I asked.

"Oh, you would not believe it. After having fun in a downtown bar, Bruno and I took a taxi, drove on a narrow road with a lot of turns, and arrived to the spectacular town of *Castelmola*. It is a medieval town perched atop a precipitous and craggy volcanic rock 2,000 feet high, right above Taormina. The town clings to that rock like a seagull perched on a flagpole. From up there Castelmola looks down on Taormina like an eagle looks at his pray. If you think Taormina has beautiful views, wait until you get up there; you really feel like being on top of the world!"

"As we wandered through tiny and steep streets up there", continued Mike, "we discovered *Bar-Turrisi*, known as Funk Bar. We enjoyed a glass of aphrodisiac wine made with almonds. But, most of all, we had so much fun there. Imagine, the entire bar is full of phallic symbols; there were wooden and ceramic penises everywhere, in the floor tiles, on the walls, on the door handles, in the light fittings, in lamp stands, in glasses, in the menu, furniture, ashtrays, chairs, clocks, etc. We were told that the place was visited by many celebrities, like Liz Taylor, Richard Burton, Burt Lancaster, and Charlton Heston. We had never seen anything like that before. Oh, boy, certainly that is not a place where I would take my grandmother! Later we took a short cut and walked back to Taormina. It was a path very tortuous, rocky, steep, and dangerous, but we loved it!"

I did not dare to ask Kelly what she did in Taormina. I am sure she had good time with Rosario. Since it was getting late, one by one, we left that moonlit terrace and went to relive the Taormina experience in our dreams!

Chapter 11

MAJESTIC MT. ETNA

Dear Reader, do you know how Mt. Etna came into existence? The ancient people had a simple explanation. *Vulcan*, god of fire, lived in a large cave under the mountain we call Etna. In the cave, he commanded a large number of blacksmiths, known as Cyclops. They forged weapons, armors, and lightning bolts. They melted also gold and silver to make jewels for gods, goddesses, and heroes.

The cave was hot and smoky all the time; it needed a chimney to release the smoke and ashes. For that purpose, Vulcan drilled a wide hole on the crust of the mountain. That explains why Mt. Etna has a hole, called crater, and why it is continuously emitting smoke. When the cave accumulated large piles of debris, Vulcan had the Cyclops shovel the debris outside through the crater. Over the many centuries, the huge amount of debris formed the volcano's slopes we see today.

Vulcan was married to *Venus*, goddess of love. Any time he discovered that she cheated on him, he became furious, and with his hammer, hit very hard the anvil, causing sparks that sat the entire cave on fire. The rocks melted, rose up from the chimney, and poured down as violent eruptions.

There is some truth in that story, because ashes and lava do come from the inner core of Earth. According to mythology, Cyclops did live on the slopes of Mt. Etna. But, that is not how Mt. Etna came into existence.

Today, volcanologists can properly explain how it was formed. No matter how we explain its origin, Mt. Etna is there with undeniable presence. It is a massive mountain virtually visible from every high point of Sicily and perpetually emitting fire and puffy clouds of smoke. It is a breathtaking wonder of the world. Sicilian people call it "Iddu" (He) or "A Muntagna" (The Mountain) as if it is a person.

The best time to see "Iddu" is when in winter and spring it is covered with a bright green, white, and red mantle. Up to about 4,000-feet the mantle is green, made of citrus groves and forest trees. Above that level, the mantle resembles a white blouse made of shining snow. On the top it has a fashionable hat made of red fire and a plume of whitish smoke. Another stunning view of Etna is given by the rising sun; it seems that little by little the mountain cloaks itself with a pink and golden dress with dazzling colors gradually descending from the summit to its flanks and base.

Like a humongous resting giant, for at least the past 500,000 years Mt. Etna has kept a watchful eye over the surrounding area. However, every now and then it has displayed a vengeful wrath and has rained down rivers of fire, lava, destruction, and death. The locals have learned to revere it and to live with its unpredictable behavior. Yes, Mt. Etna is majestic, fascinating, and frightening at the same time.

SMOKING MT. ETNA IN WINTER

My 27 enthusiast *Volcanologists* did not want to leave Sicily without getting to know his Majesty Mt. Etna and pay respects to it. Therefore, we reserved day eleven of our Sicilian Adventure just for that. At 8:30 a.m., we took the freeway direction Catania, drove by vast groves of orange and lemon trees and exited at Acireale. It was a sunny morning with temperature in the low 80s.

First we passed through a few small towns and villages where dark lava stones have been used to pave streets, build houses, erect retaining-walls, make doorways, windows, and many other kinds of constructions. The soil in that area is made of a pulverized reddish lava substance, very suitable for cultivating oranges, lemons, mandarins, olives, grape vines, lime, almonds, pears, apples, prickly pears, palms, eucalyptus, and pistachio.

Once we passed the village of Nocolosi, a long and winding road took us through a wooded area with dense bushes, oak, chestnut, beech, and pine trees. On both sides of the road, we saw bright pink and white valerian and yellow broom flowers. There we encountered a large herd of goats blocking our way. We were surprised to see also a few people riding bikes to the mountain top.

As we drove out of the wooded area and reached an elevation of about 6,000-feet, the landscape changed dramatically. The road became darker, bumpy, and scarred by recent lava flows. We saw rivers of old and discolored lava that had poured down and engulfed houses, mountain lodges, and trees. In fact, some eruptions destroyed not only houses, but entire towns lying on the Volcano's slopes. In 1183, the red lava destroyed most of the city of Catania and 15,000 people died. In 1697, 40 villages were destroyed and about 100,000 people died under the ruins. In 1928, the village of Mascali was obliterated in two days.

Next, we drove through an immense and desolate landscape completely covered with barren black lava. Only some lichen and moss can grow on those black rocks. A few small, dormant, and moon-like craters were seen in the distant valleys. That entire view was surreal, lunar, and fascinating at the same time. It seemed that we had landed on another planet. We stopped twice for pictures.

At 10:15 a.m., we drove between two large extinct volcanic craters, called *Silvestri Craters*, and arrived to *Rifugio Sapienza*, about 8,000-feet high. That marked the end of the road. The parking lot had many cars and tour buses. There were also cafes, bars, restaurants, souvenir shops, two hotels, and many tourists. As we exited the bus, we noticed that the temperature was in the mid 40s. We needed a jacket.

I gave my thrilled 27 Volcanologists free time until 3:00 p.m. They immediately headed for a coffee and a souvenir shop. Then, most of us climbed one of the dormant Silvestri Craters, made of volcanic sand and pebbles. We walked around the rim, collected a few small black rocks, and took pictures.

Then, most people in my group bought tickets for the cable car and went much higher, to the *Observation Station*, about 11,500-feet high. The sun was shining, but the air quite cold. There we stopped for a while and looked around us: we saw everywhere huge blocks of black lava, precipitous ravines, abysses and valleys covered with high walls of solidified black lava. There were also a few small dormant craters. On the far horizon down below, we could see green forests, towns, villages, and the blue Ionian Sea. It was beautiful, spectacular!

Among those ghostly volcanic rocks, we saw an enormous, lone stone that looked like a human head. It has been nicknamed *Happy Face*. A legend tells that rock was continuously complaining inside Vulcan's cave. Tired of listening to it, the god of fire kicked it out through Etna's main crater. When that miserable rock came out, breathed fresh air, saw the sunlight above, the blue sea and the green landscape below, it felt so happy that it burst into an uncontrollable laugh and has been laughing ever since!

At the Observation Station, we took a coffee break and bought a few small souvenirs. Then we boarded a large *four-wheel jeep-bus* with huge tractor tires. The jeep moved upwards through rough tracks near precipitous ravines, crevasses, and abysms. We encountered small extinct craters, rivers of lava, lava tunnels, vast fields of reddish ashes, and stunning views. We saw small puddles with dirty snow, reddish pebbles, and whitish smoke that smelled like sulfur. When we reached the summit at an altitude of about 12,500-feet, we were almost at the top of Mt. Etna. The air was thin and the temperature freezing.

A guide took us all around the rim of a large dormant crater. We walked on a narrow path of loose and burned reddish pebbles that moved under our feet. We had to walk cautiously: getting too close to the edge meant we could slip and roll all the way down to the bottom of the dormant crater!

At the end of that walk, five of us hired another guide and went to the rim of a nearby active crater. There we saw a large jet of red lava, and ashes continuously rise in the air and fall back into the same place. There were large puffs of black smoke and a stink of sulfur that smelled like sickening rotten eggs. We looked down into the belly of the crater and had a glimpse of what hell must look like. We paused for a moment and scolded the volcano for unleashing its wrath on the surroundings, so many terrifying rivers of fire and magma with temperatures higher than 3,000 degrees.

Peter insisted that he saw in the crater the ruthless barbarian *King Theodoric* desperately crying for help. The legend says that he was such a brutal king that, after death, the devil snatched his body from the tomb in Ravenna, Italy, and dropped it into the flames of the burning Mt. Etna. Is it a reality or a myth? History confirms the tomb of the Ostrogoth king was found empty right after he was buried in 526 A.D.

As we walked, we saw several small puddles of smoke billowing from the ground below our feet. We could feel the heat coming through the sole of our shoes. We could feel the heat also in our hands if we touched the ground. We picked up some dirt and a few pebbles: they were warm! On the outside flank of the crater, we saw numerous small vents and cones, like giant warts. Each of them had a plume of smoke and a sulfuric steam rising into the air.

Yes, we stood at an altitude of some 12,500-feet; we walked on the rim of an active volcano; we looked into its crater and we listened to the sound of magma boiling inside it. What an astonishing, surreal, and unforgettable experience! We saw the power of Mt. Etna and we felt to bow to his majesty. For sure, our day eleven of our Sicilian Adventure was a memorable and educational experience forever etched in our mind.

MT. ETNA: WALKING ON THE RIM OF AN EXTINCT CRATER

After our thrilling experience on top of Mt. Etna, we took the jeep-bus back to the Observation Station. From there we jumped into a cable car and descended to the parking lot. A brief stop at a couple of souvenir shops and a delicious Sicilian lunch at La Cantoniera Restaurant concluded our visit to His Majesty Mt. Etna.

At 3:00 p.m., we traveled back down on a different road. We stopped in an open area where a few foxes usually come to get food from travelers. We could see them behind bushes, shyly looking at us. We placed some food on a rock, returned to our bus, and started moving very slowly. Only then the foxes came out and got their food.

On our way back to the hotel, I heard many comments from my people. In particular I liked the one made by Tony and Paul. Tony remarked, "Why do people continue to live that close to the volcano, knowing all the destruction and death it has caused in the past?" Paul said, "This visit humbles me. The power of nature is awesome!"

I commented, "Tony, people continue to live in that dangerous area because they have the ability of turning a bad situation into a good outcome. Over hundreds of years, they have transformed the volcanic ashes into a very fertile soil. Paul, you are right, a visit to living Mt. Etna makes us realize that we are not the only breathing creatures on Earth. Etna also is a living mountain that breaths, smokes, punishes with fire, and blesses with rich soil."

Next, we visited "*Frantoio Leonardi*" (Leonardi's Oil mill) in the village of Zafferana. Although it was not the season to make olive oil, the owner, Mr. Leonardi, told us everything about it. He was also good in making soap with olive oil mixed with other local aromatic ingredients. When he explained why a particular kind of soap was labeled *aphrodisiac*, he sold all aphrodisiac soap he had! Leonardi was also an expert beekeeper; he showed us his beehives and taught us all about bees and honey making. Of course, we tasted some oil on toasted bread and some honey on a small spoon. Yes, we did buy a few jars of oil and honey.

BRUSCHETTA WITH OLIVE OIL

After dinner at Hotel Antares, we sat on the large terrace surrounded by tropical plants. There were two other tour groups, one from Germany and the other from Greece. It was a real international evening with a variety of music. The Germans were good at dancing the Polka and Waltz; the Greeks gave a lively performance of their traditional dances and we demonstrated our expertise in line-dancing. We had another evening of fun under the Sicilian full moon!

Chapter 12

COUNTRY ROAD, TAKE ME HOME!

In the morning of our last day in Sicily, we woke up to another beautiful day. As usual, the sun was brilliant, the sky radiant and the temperature perfect. I went to the breakfast room and greeted my *Good Sheep*. I noticed that they were rather sad because their trip was almost over. A few ladies asked questions about the return flight, the duty-free purchases, and the procedure through the Customs. "Please don't be concerned", I said, "We will talk about that later today. You still have one more day to enjoy your vacation. Live one more day like lions!" A few men roared like lions.

We left Hotel Antares at 8:30 a.m. and took the freeway headed north to Messina, along the Ionian coast. We drove by quaint villages and saw a few fishing boats returning with their night catch. Two large ships and a cruise liner were sailing on the horizon.

Surprisingly, *Messina* presented itself as a modern city with wide streets and recent constructions. That is due to the fact that in December 1908, within 40 seconds, the entire city was completely destroyed by a powerful earthquake and then by a 40-foot high tsunami. At least 60,000 people perished. Some of the survivors were relocated in other parts of Italy and others left for America.

By the Port of Messina, we saw a huge ferry-boat loading people, cars, trucks, and buses. Other ferry-boats were on the way to or from the town of

Villa San Giovanni in the Calabria Region, the southernmost tip of the Italian peninsula.

The *Strait of Messina* separates Sicily from mainland Italy; it is two-miles wide and 830-feet deep. In the olden times, the northern portion of the Strait was much feared by sailors, because of the very dangerous whirlpools that destroyed boats. Actually, there is a strong underwater current running from south to north and another one from north going south; the two currents meet and swirl every six hours, presenting real problems in navigation. The currents were described and personified by the Greek poet Homer as *Scylla and Charybdis*, two female sea monsters that wrecked the boats and devoured the sailors.

The city of Messina is not a tourist destination. The only thing that attracts visitors is the *Astronomical Clock*, located in the facade of the Cathedral's Bell Tower. Each day, a little before noon, spectators gather in Piazza Duomo to watch an amazing show. As the clock strikes 12, the bells chime and the show begins. A complex mechanism puts in motion gilded figures representing characters and events of the local civil and religious history. Several bronze statues begin to rotate: a rampant lion roars, moves his head and tail, and waves a flagpole with the standard of Messina; a cockerel flaps its wings and crows three times. Then begins a procession of golden statues: first, come the two Sicilian heroines Diana and Clarence, next comes the Virgin Mary, the nativity scene with shepherds, St. Joseph, the Wise Men, Easter, Pentecost, the Apostles, and a flying dove. The show ends with a melodious music playing the Ave Maria. The dazzling display lasts 12 minutes. We did see the Astronomical Clock, but could not stay for the noon show. We had a busy day already planned.

At 10:30 a.m., we took the freeway again and drove along the Tyrrhenian seashore, passing by the towns of Milazzo, Barcellona, Falcone, Oliveri, Tindari, Patti, Gioiosa Marea, and Brolo. Along the way, we saw Stromboli, a small active volcano on the Lipari Islands. We asked it to behave.

At Capo d'Orlando we took a country road and headed for the town of *Longi*. As the road began to climb, *Joseph Lazzara, Rose Zingales and Ross Miceli* started to sing, "I am going to take a sentimental journey...." They were so cheery because they were going to see the town of their family roots.

Longi is a suggestive medieval mountain town perched on a high precipice. Its inhabitants make their living cultivating wheat, olives, and grapes. The fields for cultivation are small and pebbly. They also raise cattle, cows, sheep, hogs, and horses.

After the terrible earthquake of 1908, many *Longitani* (inhabitants of Longi), having lost their homes, moved to Cleveland, Ohio. There they founded the *San Leone Club* and kept their traditions alive. Most of them never had the opportunity to see Longi again, but they told their children and grandchildren about their homeland. These kept deep in their heart the desire of visiting it someday. For the *Lazzara, Zingales, and Miceli,* their dream was about to come true.

STRAIT OF MESSINA

There was only one road into and out of Longi; it was narrow, winding, and rocky; at times it made our head spin. We had to stop twice to let a few *maiali neri* (black boars) cross the road. They breed abundantly in those mountains and their meat is delicious.

At a certain point, Tony sighed, "Oh, look at that! Captain Giuseppe, stop the bus. I want a picture with her." On a small rest area Tony had just seen a pretty farmer woman selling fresh vegetables from the back of an old pick-up truck. She had a dark blue dress, a reddish apron, and long black hair tied with a red headscarf. We stopped; a few people got off the bus and bought straw-berries, fava beans, and ricotta. Yes, Tony did have his pictures with the farmer woman, who gladly posed as if she was selling him a bundle of garlic. Tony thanked her with a kiss on the cheek.

LONGI

At the entrance of the town, my three Longitani had their picture taken by the sign *Benvenuti a Longi* (Welcome to Longi). People in there must have spotted our bus a few miles away, because when we arrived to central square, we found a least 30 cheerful individuals anxiously waiting for us. A few weeks earlier, I had informed the parish priest and the mayor of our visit; they spread the news in town.

Immediately the locals inquired, "Chi e' Lazzara?" (Who is Lazzara?), "Dov'e' mio cugino Zingales?" (Where is my cousin Zingales?), "Ross Miceli!" They had never met their American relatives. I told the rest of the group to feel free and to return to the Piazza at 1:00 p.m. I remained with my three Longitani to help with the language problem.

After the Lazzara and the Zingales showed a few old pictures, they immediately found relatives. Ross Miceli found a distant cousin who spoke some English. Many hugs were exchanged and a few tears fell. Then, I took my three Longitani and their newly found relatives to the *Municipio* (City Hall). Mayor *Leone Pidala'* received us warmly and wrote birth and marriage certificates of those people's grandparents. All employees in the Municipio were in a festive and helpful mood; they greeted us individually and enquired about their relatives in Cleveland.

Next, we moved to the medieval parish church of San Michele Arcangelo, where *Father Angelo Carcione* welcomed us, gave a tour of the church, and showed the statue of Saint Leone. My three Longitani shed a few tears and made a donation to the Church in memory of their grandparents.

89

After that, we were escorted to the humble houses where *Grandpas* Lazzara, Zingales, and Miceli lived during their youth. Some distant relatives were now living in there; they invited us in and few more tears fell in there too. A small crowd followed us wherever we went; some had messages for the relatives in Cleveland, while others just wanted to see what Americans look like.

We made a stop at the *Monumento degli Eroi* (Monument of the Heroes), which listed names of local young men who died during World War I and II. A few Lazzara and Zingales were among them. Several people invited us to stop at their home for a drink. A few invited us for lunch, but we kindly thanked them, because we had already made reservations at a local restaurant.

In the meanwhile, the rest of my flock strolled through Corso Umberto and in a few narrow and old side streets. They talked to the locals, had a drink at a bar, and visited the medieval *Castello Baronale* (Baron's Castle).

At 1:30 p.m., we boarded our bus and went to a country restaurant called *La Petrusa*. We were all hungry and anxious to taste local food. We were accompanied by Mayor Pidala', Father Angelo, and a few relatives of our three Cleveland people.

The waiters started serving an antipasto made of salami, cheese, eggplants, peppers, mushrooms, and pickled artichokes. Then we had three kinds of pasta: maccaroni with ragu' of black pig, tagliatelle alla boscaiola, pappardelle with porcini mushrooms. Fresh salad, a grilled steak of black pig, home-made bread, grapes, peeled prickly pears, coffee, and limoncello. We had all the red and white Moscato wine we wanted. Some Sicilian music made us sing and do line-dancing. Later, we called the chef and the waiters to the dining room and gave them a deafening round of applause. I am sure La Petrusa Restaurant never saw a livelier group of tourists like ours.

Later, a few men in the group kept on saying, "Mamma Mia, I cannot believe I ate that whole thing! It was so good! It was a real square meal! I never had so much fun! I am not going to eat for the next three days!" Yes, we had an unforgettable time in that little mountain town.

PASTA WITH RAGU OF BLACK PIG. HOW DELICIOUS...!

At 4:30 p.m., we bid farewell to our hosts. More hugs with relatives were exchanged and more tears shed. Then we descended through that same winding country road and finally reached the freeway by the sea coast. No one whined about the rough road on the way down: everybody was sleeping!

An hour later, I picked up the microphone and whispered, "Wake up, wake up". We took a coffee break at the picturesque town of *Santo Stefano di Camastra*, famous for its refined handmade artistic ceramic articles. "This is really your last chance to shop!" I said. We walked through the quaint Viale delle Palme, lined with colorful shops.

At our favorite Fiesta Hotel, our hosts were glad to see us back. Yes, we certainly had our last and best festival of food and fun! A Farewell Party on the large terrace under the moonlight concluded our memorable Sicilian Holiday.

Early in the morning, we loaded our baggage on the bus and Captain Giuseppe drove us to *Palermo's Airport*. On the way, I gave the necessary instructions about checking-in and boarding the plane. Then, I said, "When you get back home for the next couple of days, you will wake up at about 2:00 a.m. You will think it is time to get up, but then you will be glad to go back to your dreams. Ladies, watch your husband while sleeping: he might still be chewing the good pasta he had in Sicily or waving at some pretty woman on a balcony. Grazie. Buon Viaggio. May God bless you all." Immediately, some people began to sing, "*Arrivederci, Sicilia. Goodbye, Au revoir*". At the airport everybody hugged Captain Giuseppe and gave him a generous tip. From Palermo we flew into Rome's Fiumicino Airport.

I did not go back to USA with my Good Sheep, because I went to my hometown in the Abruzzo region and stayed a couple of weeks with my 98-year-old Mamma Lucia. When I returned home, I found many *Thank-You* notes; they said:

"It was a trip of a life time."

"You made the old country come alive."

"Sicily has become part of my life."

"It was a dream trip."

"Great time and a lot of laughs. Grazie."

"We enjoyed every single bit of it."

"I will never forget it. It was a blast."

"This was the most enjoyable tour. We had a great time."

"I am so grateful for the beautiful memories of Sicily etched in my heart."

My Dear People, Grazie, Thank You, Merci, Danke, Gracias.

TRINACRIA: SYMBOL OF ANCIENT SICILY

CPSIA information can be obtained
at www.ICGtesting.com
Printed in the USA
BVHW022005250721
612699BV00001B/1